knowledge and the
social sciences

AN INTRODUCTION TO THE SOCIAL SCIENCES: UNDERSTANDING SOCIAL CHANGE

This book is part of a series produced in association with The Open University. The complete list of books in the series is as follows:

Questioning Identity: Gender, Class, Ethnicity
edited by Kath Woodward

The Natural and the Social: Uncertainty, Risk, Change
edited by Steve Hinchliffe and Kath Woodward

Ordering Lives: Family, Work and Welfare
edited by Gordon Hughes and Ross Fergusson

A Globalizing World? Culture, Economics, Politics
edited by David Held

Knowledge and the Social Sciences: Theory, Method, Practice
edited by David Goldblatt

The books form part of the Open University courses DD100 and DD121/ DD122 *An Introduction to the Social Sciences: Understanding Social Change.* Details of these and other Open University courses can be obtained from the Course Information and Advice Centre, PO Box 724, The Open University, Milton Keynes MK7 6ZS, United Kingdom: tel. +44 (0)1908 653231, e-mail general-enquiries@open.ac.uk

Alternatively, you may visit the Open University website at http://www.open.ac.uk where you can learn more about the wide range of courses and packs offered at all levels by The Open University.

For availability of other course components visit the webshop at www.ouw.co.uk, or contact Open University Worldwide, Michael Young Building, Walton Hall, Milton Keynes MK7 6AA, United Kingdom for a brochure. tel. +44 (0)1908 858785; fax +44 (0)1908 858787; e-mail ouwenq@open.ac.uk

knowledge and the
social sciences:
theory, method, practice

edited by david goldblatt

London and New York

in association with

The Open
University

First published 2000 by Routledge; written and produced by The Open University
Second edition 2004
11 New Fetter Lane, London EC4P 4EE

Simultaneously published in the USA and Canada by Routledge
29 West 35th Street, New York, NY 10001

Routledge is an imprint of the Taylor & Francis Group

This text has been printed on paper produced in Sweden from wood from managed forests using an elemental chlorine-free bleaching process. It has been stated as being environmentally friendly by the Swedish Association for the Protection of Nature.

Edited, designed and typeset by The Open University.

Printed in the United Kingdom by The Bath Press, Bath.

British Library Cataloguing in Publication Data
A catalogue record for this book is available from The British Library

Library of Congress Cataloging in Publication Data
A catalogue record for this book has been requested

ISBN 0-415-32975-2 (hbk)

ISBN 0-415-32976-0 (pbk)

ISBN 0-203-39220-5 (ebk)

2.1

Contents

The Open University course team

John Allen, *Professor of Geography*

Penny Bennett, *Editor*

Pam Berry, *Compositor*

Simon Bromley, *Senior Lecturer in Government*

Lydia Chant, *Course Manager*

Stephen Clift, *Editor*

Allan Cochrane, *Professor of Public Policy*

Lene Connolly, *Print Buying Controller*

Jonathan Davies, *Graphic Designer*

Graham Dawson, *Lecturer in Economics*

Alison Edwards, *Editor*

Ross Fergusson, *Staff Tutor in Social Policy*

Fran Ford, *Senior Course Co-ordination Secretary*

Ian Fribbance, *Staff Tutor in Economics*

David Goldblatt, *Co-Course Team Chair*

Richard Golden, *Production and Presentation Administrator*

Jenny Gove, *Lecturer in Psychology*

Peter Hamilton, *Lecturer in Sociology*

Celia Hart, *Picture Researcher*

David Held, *Professor of Politics and Sociology*

Susan Himmelweit, *Professor of Economics*

Stephen Hinchliffe, *Lecturer in Geography*

Wendy Hollway, *Professor of Psychology*

Gordon Hughes, *Senior Lecturer in Social Policy*

Wendy Humphreys, *Staff Tutor in Government*

Jonathan Hunt, *Co-publishing Advisor*

Christina Janoszka, *Course Manager*

Pat Jess, *Staff Tutor in Geography*

Bob Kelly, *Staff Tutor in Government*

Margaret Kiloh, *Staff Tutor in Social Policy*

Sylvia Lay-Flurrie, *Secretary*

Gail Lewis, *Senior Lecturer in Social Policy*

Siân Lewis, *Graphic Designer*

Liz McFall, *Lecturer in Sociology*

Tony McGrew, *Professor of International Relations, University of Southampton*

Hugh Mackay, *Staff Tutor in Sociology*

Maureen Mackintosh, *Professor of Economics*

Eugene McLaughlin, *Senior Lecturer in Criminology and Social Policy*

Andrew Metcalf, *Senior Producer, BBC*

Gerry Mooney, *Staff Tutor in Social Policy*

Lesley Moore, *Senior Course Co-ordination Secretary*

Ray Munns, *Graphic Artist*

Karim Murji, *Senior Lecturer in Sociology*

Sarah Neal, *Lecturer in Social Policy*

Kathy Pain, *Staff Tutor in Geography*

Clive Pearson, *Tutor Panel*

Ann Phoenix, *Professor of Psychology*

Lynn Poole, *Tutor Panel*

Raia Prokhovnik, *Senior Lecturer in Government*

Norma Sherratt, *Staff Tutor in Sociology*

Roberto Simonetti, *Lecturer in Economics*

Dick Skellington, *Project Officer*

Brenda Smith, *Staff Tutor in Psychology*

Mark Smith, *Senior Lecturer in Government*

Matt Staples, *Course Manager*

Grahame Thompson, *Professor of Political Economy*

Ken Thompson, *Professor of Sociology*

Diane Watson, *Staff Tutor in Sociology*

Stuart Watt, *Lecturer in Psychology*

Andy Whitehead, *Graphic Artist*

Kath Woodward, *Course Team Chair, Senior Lecturer in Sociology*

Chris Wooldridge, *Editor*

External Assessor

Nigel Thrift, *Professor of Geography, University of Oxford*

Series preface

Knowledge and the Social Sciences: Theory, Method, Practice is the fifth in
a series of five books, entitled *An Introduction to the Social Sciences:
Understanding Social Change*. If the social sciences are to retain and extend
their relevance in the twenty-first century there can be little doubt that they
will have to help us understand social change. In the 1990s an introductory
course to the social sciences would have looked completely different.

From a global perspective it appears that the pace of change is quickening,
social and political ideas and institutions are under threat. The international
landscape has changed; an intensification of technological change across
computing, telecommunications, genetics and biotechnology present new
political, cultural and moral dilemmas and opportunities. Real intimations of a
global environmental crisis in the making have emerged. We are, it appears,
living in an uncertain world. We are in new territory.

The same is also true of more local concerns. At the beginning of the twenty-
first century both societies and the social sciences are in a state of flux.
Understanding Social Change has been written at a moment that reflects,
albeit in a partial way, subterranean shifts in the social and cultural character
of the UK. Established social divisions and social identities of class, gender,
ethnicity and nation are fragmenting and re-forming. Core institutions such as
the family, work and welfare have become more diverse and complex. It is
also a moment when significant processes of change have been set in train –
such as constitutional reform and European economic and monetary
union – whose longer-term trajectory remains uncertain. The flux in the
social sciences has been tumultuous. Social change, uncertainty and diversity
have rendered many of the most well-established frameworks in the social
sciences of limited use and value. Social change on this scale demands fresh
perspectives and new systems of explanation.

In this context *Understanding Social Change* is part of a bold and innovative
educational project, for it attempts to capture and explore these processes of
momentous social change and in doing so reasserts the utility and necessity of
the social sciences. Each of the five books which make up the series attempts
precisely this, and they all do so from a fundamentally interdisciplinary
perspective. Social change is no respecter of the boundaries of disciplines and
the tidy boxes that social scientists have often tried to squeeze it into. Above
all, *Understanding Social Change* seeks to maintain and extend the Open
University's democratic educational mission: to reach and enthuse an
enormously diverse student population; to insist that critical, informed,
reflexive engagement with the direction of social change is not a matter for
elites and professional social scientists alone.

As you may have guessed, this series of books forms a core component of the Open University, Faculty of Social Sciences, level 1 course, DD100 *An Introduction to the Social Sciences: Understanding Social Change*. Each book in the series can be read independently of the other books and independently from the rest of the materials that make up the Open University course. However, if you wish to use the series as a whole, there are a number of references to chapters in other books in the series, and these are easily identifiable because they are printed in bold type.

Making the course and these books has been a long and complex process, and thanks are due to an enormous number of people.

First and foremost, the entire project has been managed and kept on the rails, when it was in mortal danger of flying off them, by our excellent Course Manager, Christina Janoszka. In the DD100 office, Fran Ford, Lesley Moore and Sylvia Lay-Flurrie have been the calm eye at the centre of a turbulent storm, our thanks to all of them. For the second edition we have had the much valued support of Matt Staples and Lydia Chant.

Stephen Clift, Chris Wooldridge and Penny Bennett have been meticulous, hawk-eyed editors. Siân Lewis has provided superb design work, and Ray Munns and Andy Whitehead have provided skilled cartographic and artistic work. David Calderwood and then Richard Golden in project control have arranged and guided the schedule with calm efficiency and Celia Hart has provided great support with illustrations and photographs. Nigel Thrift, our external assessor, and Clive Pearson, Elizabeth Chaplin and Lynne Poole, our tutor panel, provided consistent and focused criticism, support and advice. Peggotty Graham has been an invaluable friend of *Understanding Social Change* and David Held provided balance, perspective and insight as only he can.

It only remains for us to say that we hope you find *Understanding Social Change* an engaging and illuminating introduction to the social sciences, and in turn you find the social sciences essential for understanding life in the twenty-first century.

David Goldblatt
Kath Woodward
Co-Chairs, The Open University Course Team

Introduction

David Goldblatt

There is a bridge over the Grand Union Canal as it heads for the Paddington Basin in west London, where you can see extraordinary sunsets. All the more extraordinary for the lack of uncluttered sky and views in the rest of the area. Crossing it at sundown with Molly, my daughter, we stopped to look at the last of the sun and its hazy red and orange streaks. I found myself repeating my mother's words to me. 'Red sky at night, shepherd's delight. Red sky in the morning, shepherds warning'. To which Molly replied, 'How'd you know that, Daddy?' As is often the case with her questions I found myself uncertain as to how to reply: because that's what my mother told me; because transport policies in London are mad and mean that all the cars' pollution produce amazing atmospheric effects; because there is some meteorological and physical connection between sky colour and weather patterns. Rather than get myself stuck in an explanation that was either unsatisfactory or beyond what I do know, I opted for a question back: 'Do you know what a shepherd is?' And then we were off into a conversation about animals and farming.

What is knowledge?

The point of the story above is not to illustrate the importance of diversionary tactics for parents – useful knowledge and skill as it is – but to illustrate how diverse is the range of knowledge that we draw upon in everyday life. I was recounting traditional, unquestioned knowledge that I had learnt as a child. I had the option of drawing on my knowledge of environmental issues and social science explanations of environmental problems. I thought I might be able to draw on a natural scientific explanation. Perhaps, in another context, someone might have opted for a more religious explanation that invoked gods or spirits to explain the colour of the sky and its consequences for the weather and for shepherds. But more than this diversity of types of knowledge, or fields of knowledge, the story illustrates other more complex forms of diversity. For example, knowledge can be held in the mind of individuals or it can be embodied in physical form. I don't carry all the details of the world's meteorological knowledge around in my head, but if I wanted to go and look at it I would find it in books, journals, web pages and so on. Knowledge can be highly explicit and theoretical. I certainly possessed an explicit, organized knowledge of transport policies and their consequences for the environment, structured by the theoretical arguments of the social sciences. On the other hand, knowledge can be tacit. I have never read or learnt any body of conversational techniques with children, but I have talked with them enough to know the use of changing the subject when things get complicated. In a similar vein, although knowledge can be simply accumulated and organized information, it is not always just this. We can think of knowledge as a body of skills, practices and understandings that we possess and use in practical ways, in other words, knowing by doing rather than knowing by thinking or by reasoning.

In *Knowledge and the Social Sciences*, we argue that the first precondition of an effective engagement by the social sciences with the world of knowledge is a recognition of the plurality and diversity of knowledges. In Chapter 1, Kath Woodward and Stuart Watt look at science, medicine and lay or 'common-sense' knowledges about illness, disease and healing. In Chapter 2, Ken Thompson and Kath Woodward look at religious knowledges. In Chapter 3, Simon Bromley takes the dominant political ideologies of the modern era as his subject of inquiry, while in Chapter 4, Kath Woodward, David Goldblatt and Liz McFall look at the impact of economic, technological and environmental knowledge in shaping patterns of change in modern societies. What unites all of these chapters' understandings of knowledge is that they are socially produced or constructed.

How is knowledge socially constructed?

At one level this is a crude sociological truism. All knowledge is produced, collected, collated and disseminated by human beings living in societies. Our intention in this book is to move beyond this truism to explore more precisely how societies shape the production of knowledge, the beliefs its members hold or reject, and the relative status, importance and validity of different types of knowledge at different times. In Chapter 1, the short account of the origins and development of the natural sciences and modern medical science illustrates just how variable knowledge of the same field can be across societies and across historical periods. But more than that, it explores the social and institutional context of the production and evaluation of knowledge. For example, how was it that medical science, even when of dubious practical value, came to displace earlier folk knowledges? Who has the power to influence which knowledge counts?

Three key elements of the social construction of knowledge are explored in this book:

- the role of language and discourse
- the role of institutions
- the role of different types of social power.

Language is a social phenomenon and no description or explanation of the world can be created without recourse to it. But the language we inherit shapes what it is we see in the world and what we cannot see, what we know and what we cannot know. When it snows I just see snow. If I think hard about it I might see sleet. But an Inuit living in Northern Canada, whose language includes over a dozen different words for snow, will see a much more precise, complex and nuanced snowstorm than I will ever see. Physicians whose knowledge of the body and illness is rooted in the language of theory of humours are unlikely to be able to recognize the importance of microbiology in causing illness. They are almost certain to explain illness in terms of humours.

Institutions are equally important in shaping the content and standing of knowledge systems. At one extreme, the dominance and public legitimacy of knowledge systems has been backed up and underscored by the use of force, terror and censorship. But even in the context of more diverse, open and plural societies, institutions exert powerful effects. They determine, for example, who has access to specialized knowledge languages (like medical training) and who has socially sanctioned and legal authority to make pronouncements on a given subject. It is clear that doctors' own institutional control of access to medical schools and the content of their curriculum, as well as editorship of key research journals, ensures that conventional medicine remains mainstream knowledge and aromatherapy appears beyond the pale. Similarly it is laws and state regulation that underwrite doctors' powers to sign you off from work or prescribe drugs on the basis of their medical knowledge. The higher status of conventional medicine over aromatherapy and homeopathy is, in part, attributable to the continuing power, influence and prestige of the established medical institutions and authorities. Which brings us to power. The production, dissemination and legitimization of knowledge requires access to and use of resources: economic, political and cultural and, as the examples above suggest, these resources are rarely equally distributed.

Chapter 1 explores all of these issues in relation to medicine, while the significance of the institutional production of knowledge is explored further in Chapter 2 in relation to religious knowledge. In Chapter 3, the account given of the production of new environmental knowledge about global warming and climate change alerts us to a further social factor that shapes knowledge – change. In the modern world, at any rate, knowledge is not static; it is forced to respond to changing circumstances and problems. In this case, the emergence of a potential global environmental catastrophe is forcing political ideologies of all kinds to reconsider their accuracy and worth.

Has there been a decline in trust in expert knowledge?

It is this sense of changing knowledges in changing times that underwrites the third key question of *Knowledge and the Social Sciences*, for across all the chapters a similar narrative is explored. In the UK following the Second World

War, and in other Western societies, it appears that there have been important shifts in the social standing and authority of many dominant knowledge systems. To put it crudely, four or five decades ago the expert knowledge held by scientists and doctors about the natural world, by politicians and bureaucrats about the social world, by religious leaders and their institutions about the moral world were held in general to be correct. Expert knowledge in all its forms was broadly respected and trusted and although none of these knowledge systems ever went completely unchallenged, their authority and social standing seemed secure. Each of the chapters in *Knowledge and the Social Sciences* explores an aspect of decline. Chapter 1 looks at how the authority of medical science has been challenged by both social scientific critiques of its neutrality and objectivity and by the alternative frameworks of thinking developed by complementary and alternative medical practices. In Chapter 2, the decline of religious knowledge is linked to both secularization and the rise of alternative spiritual and belief systems. Chapter 3 explores how mainstream political ideologies – liberalism, socialism and conservatism – have been forced to reconsider many of their core explanatory and normative assumptions by both the threat of environmental degradation and the alternative arguments and positions of environmentalism and the green movement. Finally in Chapter 4, the emergence of new forms of expertise is explored in relation to some of the different ways in which knowledge is transmitted and produced in contemporary societies and at the shift in focus from production to consumption in understanding changing economic systems. In each case the decline in trust is not assumed but explored, and the certainties of the past are critically interrogated. Above all, the uncertainties of these dominant forms of knowledge are set in the context of a society where knowledge is increasingly diverse and complex.

Can knowledge produce social change?

It is the impact of diverse and plural knowledge systems that brings us to our fourth guiding question. For most of the above is concerned with how societies shape knowledge – its production, status and so on. But it should be clear that the relationship can work in the other direction. Knowledge itself can have major social effects. This is the core of the case made by the advocates of the *knowledge society*, the *consumer society* and the *risk society*, which are explored and compared in depth in Chapter 4. Although these theories of social change in modern societies differ in many ways, they all agree that the types of knowledge we are now producing and the ways in which it is disseminated and used are having structural effects in the societies in which we live. Access to knowledge can make us richer or poorer, more secure or more insecure, more socially harmonious or divided. Which way we go as a society remains open, but change is on the way.

The social sciences as a form of knowledge?

What, then, is the place of the social sciences in all of this? For if they are nothing else, the social sciences are a systematic and organized body of concepts, theories, information and evidence about the social world. How are the social sciences produced, what are their institutional contexts and origins? What guarantees their worth and legitimacy and can they effect social change? We will return to some of these questions in the Afterword to this book. But first we must get a clearer sense of the epistemological and methodological underpinnings of the social sciences. Each chapter in *Knowledge and the Social Sciences* addresses one aspect of this. In Chapter 1, the role of social sciences and social explanations of illness and health is contrasted with that of the natural sciences and some of the difficulties and virtues of combining social scientific and medical thinking are explored. In Chapter 2, alongside the exploration of religious change in the UK since the Second World War, there is an explicit attempt to look at the different ways in which various traditions within the social sciences explore the same social phenomena. In particular, the chapter compares and contrasts *positivist* and *interpretative* models of the social sciences, with their differing emphasis on the types of evidence they use, the evaluation and organization of that evidence and the standing and testing of claims and theories. In Chapter 3, the political ideologies of our era – a specialized and specific element of the social sciences – are examined. The chapter illustrates the central role of moral and normative values in shaping what social scientists look at, how they explain the world and what vision of its future they might have. Finally, in Chapter 4, we look at different social science approaches to the 'knowledge revolution', weighing up the advantages and disadvantages of this transformation and the extent to which social changes in knowledge production create greater democracy or increased anxiety.

Science and society: knowledge in medicine

Kath Woodward and Stuart Watt

Contents

1 INTRODUCTION

What counts as knowledge? What do we mean when we say that we know something? What is the status of different kinds of knowledge? In order to explore these questions we are going to focus on one particular area of knowledge – medicine.

How do you *know* when you are ill? This may seem to be an absurd question. You know you are ill because you *feel* ill; your body tells you that you are ill. You may know that you feel pain or discomfort but *knowing* you are ill is a bit more complex. At times, people experience the symptoms of illness, but in fact they are simply tired or over-worked or they may just have a hangover. At other times, people may be suffering from a disease and fail to be aware of the illness until it has reached a late stage in its development. So how do we *know* we are ill, and what counts as knowledge?

Think about this example. You feel unwell. You have a bad cough and always seem to be tired. Perhaps it could be stress at work, or maybe you should give up smoking. You feel worse. You visit the doctor who listens to your chest and heart, takes your temperature and blood pressure, and then finally prescribes antibiotics for your cough.

Things do not improve but you struggle on thinking you should pull yourself together, perhaps things will ease off at work soon. A return visit to your doctor shocks you. This time the doctor, drawing on years of training and experience, diagnoses pneumonia. This means that you will need bed rest and a considerable time off work. The scenario is transformed. Although you still have the same symptoms, you no longer think that these are caused by pressure at work. You now have proof that you are ill. This is the result of the combination of your own subjective experience and the diagnosis of someone who has the status of a medical expert. You have a medically authenticated diagnosis and it appears that you are seriously ill; you know you are ill and have evidence upon which to base this knowledge.

ACTIVITY 1.1

How many examples of different sources of knowledge does the above scenario offer? Can you find examples of personal knowledge, of knowledge of one's own body, of expert knowledge and of pharmaceutical knowledge?

Where do you think these different knowledges might come from?

COMMENT _____

This scenario shows many different sources of knowledge. For example, you decide to consult the doctor in the first place because you feel unwell – this is personal knowledge about your own body. However, the doctor's expert diagnosis is based on experience and training, with sources of knowledge as diverse as other experts, laboratory reports, medical textbooks and years of experience.

This example shows some of the different sources of knowledge we draw upon when seeking to know about health and illness; even to knowing whether or not we are ill. But how is this medical knowledge produced?

One source of knowledge is the experience of our own bodies; the personal knowledge we have of changes that might be significant, as well as the subjective experience of pain and physical distress. These experiences are mediated by other forms of knowledge such as the words we have available to describe our experience and the common sense of our families and friends as well as that drawn from popular culture. Over the past decade, for example, Western culture has seen a significant emphasis on stress-related illness in the media. Reference to being 'stressed out' has become a common response in daily exchanges in the workplace and has become part of popular common-sense knowledge. It is thus not surprising that we might seek such an explanation of physical symptoms of discomfort.

We might also rely on the observations of others who know us. Comments from friends and family such as 'you do look ill' or 'that's a bad cough' might be another source of knowledge. Complementary health practices, such as holistic medicine, produce their own sets of knowledge upon which we might also draw in deciding the nature and degree of our ill health and about possible treatments.

Perhaps the most influential and authoritative source of knowledge is the medical knowledge provided by the general practitioner. We expect the doctor to have access to expert knowledge. This is socially sanctioned. It would not be acceptable to notify our employer that we simply *felt* too unwell to turn up for work or that our faith healer, astrologer, therapist or even our priest thought it was not a good idea. We need an expert medical diagnosis in order to obtain the necessary certificate if we need to be off work for more than the statutory self-certification period. The knowledge of the medical sciences is privileged in this respect in contemporary Western culture. Medical practitioners are also seen as having the required expert knowledge that permits them legally to prescribe drugs and treatment to which patients would not otherwise have access. However, there is a range of different knowledges upon which we draw when making decisions about our own state of health.

However, there is more than existing knowledge in this little story; new knowledge is constructed within it. Given the doctor's medical training and background, she may hypothesize 'is this now pneumonia?' and then proceed to look for evidence about it. She will use observations and instruments to assess the evidence and – critically – interpret it in the light of her training and experience. This results in new knowledge and new experience both for you and for the doctor. This will then be added to the doctor's medical knowledge and may help in future diagnosis of pneumonia.

Another source of knowledge here is the language and practices that create knowledge. The specialist language of the doctor produces meaning that has medically recognized status. Pneumonia is classified as a serious illness. It can be diagnosed according to an agreed set of symptoms. It has status in medical discourse as an illness. Part of the doctor's authority rests on having privileged access to specialist language and classificatory systems. However, such language is increasingly entering into the discourses of common sense, for example, medical scientific research into stress-related illness has been popularized in everyday discourse. There is overlap but there are still boundaries between medical and scientific knowledge and what we have called common-sense knowledge. What might privilege the knowledge of medical science in defining illness? How do we distinguish medical science as an example of a scientific way of thinking and as a particular knowledge system? How is medical knowledge produced? Which knowledge counts and who has authority to validate what counts as medical knowledge? This chapter uses the example of medicine as illustrative of scientific knowledge to explore the social production of knowledge and the diversity of knowledge systems.

SUMMARY

Our example of medical knowledge illustrates the following.

- The need to ask questions; looking for evidence regarding those questions, interpreting this evidence and using this interpretation to act, and to change your understanding of the world.

- Many different sources of evidence may be used.

- Authority is an essential element of expert medical knowledge.

- Expert knowledge is socially sanctioned in a way that common-sense knowledge is usually not.

- All knowledge requires some social expression and socially accepted meaning, but some has more status than others.

2 KNOWLEDGE IN MEDICINE AND SCIENCE

What distinguishes medical science as a field of knowledge or set of knowledges?

Part of what distinguishes the patient from the doctor in the previous section is that the doctor has specialized medical knowledge that the patient lacks. This specialized knowledge is a collection of evidence and theories about our bodies, experience of diseases, how we respond to them and about how they can best be treated. But the general public also has knowledge of medicine – a 'common-sense' knowledge that is of a rather different kind. Significantly, doctors' knowledge is marked by their having a licence to practise medicine. This gives them a social authority in the field of medicine that we – along with our faith healer, astrologer, therapist and priest – do not. So, has this special authority attached to the medical knowledge of professional physicians always been there, and if not, how has medical knowledge changed so that some is more valuable than the rest?

BOX 1.1   Medicine through the ages

This example shows how some acceptable approaches to medicine have evolved over the years.

Patient to Healer: I have an earache.

Healer in 2000 BC: Eat this root.

Healer in 1000 AD: That root is heathen medicine. Say this prayer.

Healer in 1850 AD: That prayer is superstition. Drink this potion.

Healer in 1940 AD: That potion is snake oil. Swallow this pill.

Healer in 2000 AD: That pill is artificial. Eat this root.

Source: Adapted from *New Scientist*, 6 September 1997

Even in ancient times, experts in medicine used their specialized knowledge to practise with drugs, surgery and a systematic and complex combination of prayers and spells, suggesting a link between science and religion. In the West for example, in the fifth century BC, medicine lost its religious and magical elements, and became more like what we today would call a science. At this time the Greek Hippocrates and others, drawing on Egyptian and near-Eastern medical practices, produced classifications of symptoms and objective accounts of ill health. Diseases were believed to have natural causes, resulting from an imbalance between four 'humours' or bodily fluids, perhaps caused by the seasons or the elements (see Figure 1.1). Physicians too changed; they needed knowledge of medicine, but also of logic, physics and even ethics – the sciences of the day.

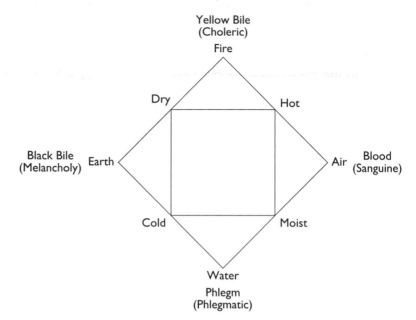

FIGURE 1.1   Interaction between the elements, weather and disease in classical medicine

This provided a forum for the development of Western medical science, which has been characterized by the establishment of socially sanctioned authority. Charles II founded the Royal Society in 1662 as an institution which allowed 'gentlemen' (and other men if they were invited, but no women) to discuss nature, philosophy and medicine separately from politics and religion. In practice, the Royal Society added two important elements to knowledge – a community, and claims to objectivity. This made knowledge produced within the Society more valuable and more authoritative, because it was believed to be more likely true than knowledge derived through other means. **Subjective knowledge** was seen as not as strong as **objective knowledge**, because it could not be confirmed by this community. Knowledge of the world was considered authoritative if it had been discussed at Society meetings or, even better, published in its journal, *Philosophical Transactions*.

The strength of this knowledge was largely due to its 'gentlemanly' origins. It was knowledge endorsed by the community of the Society and its members – the only audience and the only judges of this knowledge – who, by virtue of their independent economic status and high social position, were believed to be free of subjective biases. What constituted a 'gentleman' was changing during this time, but being male was still a requirement, as was possessing the right manners and character. Many, like Edmund Stone (see Box 1.2), were clergymen.

Subjective knowledge Knowledge that depends on one person's personal experience.

Objective knowledge Knowledge which it is claimed is completely independent of whoever happens to describe and classify it.

BOX 1.2   **Willow bark and marsh fever**

In 1763, the Reverend Edmund Stone of Chipping Norton in Oxfordshire, looked at willow bark, and investigated whether it could help alleviate the marsh fever that was common in the area. He had three reasons for looking at the bark of the white willow (*Salix alba*). First, its taste reminded him of 'Peruvian bark' (cinchona, a source of quinine) which was used to treat malaria. Second, there was 'the general maxim, that many natural maladies carry their cures along with them, or that their remedies lie not far from their causes'. And finally, for Stone, 'the intention of Providence' in this link between the causes of illness and their remedies was also an influential factor.

Stone gave willow bark to about fifty people who had the symptoms of rheumatic fever, and found that it did seem to help. His report was published in the Royal Society's *Philosophical Transactions*, but it was more or less ignored.

It is now known that salicin, the active ingredient in willow bark, has a similar effect to (and is related to) aspirin. Aspirin also had a herbal origin – it was derived from meadowsweet (*Spirea ulmaria*), which was also known to folk medicine as a pain reliever. Aspirin was patented in 1900, and has since become the most popular drug of all time.

ACTIVITY 1.2

What do you think the above example tells us about knowledge?

What kinds of knowledge was Stone drawing on in this work? What do you think he was producing?

Was he being objective?

COMMENT _____

Stone gave three reasons for investigating willow bark: reasons as diverse as his sense of taste, his knowledge of 'common-sense' medicine, and his biblical knowledge and religious faith. With these, and the evidence that he gathered and interpreted, he produced what was called *scientific* knowledge that willow bark was beneficial in alleviating the symptoms of marsh fever.

His interpretation of the evidence seems to have been affected by the expectations set up by, for example, his religious faith. It is difficult to disentangle the objective and the subjective. This is a general problem with scientific studies of medical treatments, an issue we will return to shortly.

Within the community of the Royal Society, new theories and methods could be brought into the field of medicine. It opened the door to new methods of gathering and using evidence that aimed to ensure that knowledge was more likely to be true. A systematic approach, open to new ideas, was badly needed in medicine. It didn't seem possible to provide strong evidence – even proof – that a particular treatment was helping, and weak evidence (such as that provided by Edmund Stone) was not enough to convince the sceptics. The new methods offered the possibility of a scientific medicine, where knowledge of medicine was distinctly more authoritative and reliable than had been the case previously. This was because the new science and the new methods it embodied within communities like the Royal Society seemed to show a way of finding knowledge that could be supported with reliable evidence.

Medical knowledge had been changing through the ages, often quite radically, but there were few clear signs of progress. Mystical and religious influences on medical knowledge have come and gone, and come again. Yet there have always been physicians with expert medical knowledge, compared to the common-sense medical knowledge of lay people. Areas of practice and experience were still excluded. Women's knowledge, especially, was often devalued and relegated to folk medicine, in spite of women's extensive experience of midwifery and healing. Despite the new science, common sense continued to be hugely influential in medicine. Elements of folk wisdom, such as the ideas that remedies are often found close by the causes of maladies and 'like cures like', remained important principles in medicine even into this century.

The core aspects of medical science knowledge that developed were:

- medical science has particular areas of concern that are investigated
- it employs particular methodologies, for example experimentation or observation
- it is characterized by dichotomies or dualisms, for example nature/culture, rational/emotional, physical/mental, objective/subjective
- science can privilege one side of these dualisms, in particular that of objectivity over subjectivity and the rational over the emotional
- methodologies adopted in scientific endeavours are designed to find out the truth, assuming that the main aim of science is to uncover truth and to make new discoveries.

2.1 Homeopathy, proof and the construction of scientific debate

The new scientific method seemed to offer the possibility of proof – of producing knowledge that was known to be true. It encouraged people to be impartial and objective observers of the world.

Science (as the knowledge and methods developed in communities like the Royal Society came to be known) gave people a number of tools they could use when looking for **proof**. These tools included being an impartial and objective observer, conducting experiments to gather evidence, using logic to reason in a sound manner with that evidence, and trying to understand the

Science
A set of techniques that seem to offer a way of producing objective and reliable knowledge of the world.
Proof
A very strong case that something is true and accurate, at least beyond all reasonable doubt.

patterns behind the way the world behaves. Together, objectivity, experiments and logic seemed to offer a way of moving beyond common sense. Given this, how can scientists find proof?

To look at this in a bit more detail, let's look at a particularly controversial example: the case of homeopathy (Schiff, 1995). Homeopathy is a form of alternative medicine that was founded in the eighteenth century by Samuel Hahnemann, based on the principle that 'like cures like', using treatments such as arsenic against diseases that have symptoms similar to arsenic poisoning. However, instead of administering arsenic directly, he would dilute it many times and shake it. Typically, a treatment like arsenic would be diluted so that one part of arsenic was present with 1,000,000,000,000,000,000,000,000,000,000 (that's 10^{30}) parts of water before being administered. In fact, Hahnemann believed that the more dilute the treatment, the more powerful the remedy! Much of the appeal of Hahnemann's approach was, and still is, his rejection of the use of powerful drugs and chemicals.

FIGURE 1.2   Homeopathic consultation at the Homoeopathy Centre, Dudley

Hahnemann took this traditional medical maxim of 'like cures like', and turned it into a central part of his theory of medicine. This maxim was not a new one – it was part of orthodox medicine at that time (except that treatments tended to be chemically strong) and it was also part of folk medicine (as the earlier marsh fever example showed). However, Hahnemann turned these two principles – 'like cures like' and the smaller the dose, the more powerful the treatment – into **laws** of medicine.

Laws in science claim to be accurate and reliable. They are never broken unless the law is incorrect or doesn't exist. There are no exceptions to

Laws
Statements about the world which always hold, and can be taken to be reliable in all instances.

scientific laws. By casting these principles as scientific laws, Hahnemann turned homeopathy into a scientific medicine that could be evaluated using properly controlled studies, experiments and observations to provide proof of whether or not these laws held.

The real problem for homeopathy began in the twentieth century when physicists managed to measure the number of atoms in a given amount of material. Put simply, at most dilutions it was almost certain that there would not be even a single atom of the original chemical left in the final treatment – which would, therefore, be only pure water. According to the laws of physics, then, homeopathy was simply impossible! The conflict between physics and homeopathy crystallized in 1988, when a group of scientists working for INSERM, the French National Institute for Health and Medical Research, published a paper claiming to show clear evidence that homeopathy worked; that substances at extremely high dilutions could affect living human cells. This article was published in the scientific journal *Nature*, perhaps the most prestigious scientific journal at the time.

Fundamentally, the processes by which articles are published has not changed since the founding of the Royal Society. In most academic journals, articles are submitted to peer review. The article is reviewed by a panel of fairly senior and expert academics in the field who advise the journal's editor whether to accept or to reject it for publication. Rejection may be for many different reasons: some articles aren't considered original enough or the methods used to gather evidence might not be reliable enough. Particularly relevant to this case, however, an article's being either unbelievable or its results not conforming to current theory are not usually grounds for rejection. Accordingly, the French scientists' article was printed in *Nature*, but with the following unprecedented footnote.

EDITORIAL RESERVATION

Readers of this article may share the incredulity of the many referees who have commented on several versions of it during the past several months. The essence of the result is that an aqueous solution of an antibody retains its ability to evoke a biological response even when diluted to such an extent that there is a negligible chance of there being a single molecule in any sample. There is no physical basis for such an activity. With the kind collaboration of Professor Benveniste, *Nature* has therefore arranged for independent investigators to observe repetitions of the experiments. A report of this investigation will appear shortly.

(*Nature*, 30 June 1988, p.818)

One month later, the report of this investigation was published, again in *Nature*. This report, entitled '"High-dilution" experiments a delusion', was written by the investigating team, which consisted of the physicist John Maddox (the then editor of *Nature*), James Randi, a magician and celebrated debunker of experiments on paranormal phenomena, and Walter W. Stewart, a physicist who specialized in detecting scientific fraud.

This debate offers an interesting insight into the actual practices of scientists. Scientists' beliefs and intuitions, their common-sense knowledge and the scientific tradition in which they have been trained, do influence their objectivity as they work to understand the world. The editor of *Nature*, a physicist by training, says of homeopathy: 'there is no *physical* basis for such an activity' (our emphasis). For Maddox's team, the sciences form a hierarchy, where more fundamental sciences, like physics, offer knowledge that is more authoritative than the knowledge produced by the more recent sciences, like biology. The backgrounds of Maddox's investigating team show physics taking precedence over medicine in this way.

In practice, the main criticism the 'fraud squad' made was that not all the experiments carried out by the French team were properly **blinded**. This technically means that the people involved – in particular the physician and the patients – should not know whether they are getting real treatment or a placebo (something thought to be innocuous, the equivalent of peppermint tea). The structure of a properly blinded study is shown in Figure 1.3.

Blinded
Experimental methods where the participants are not aware of the actual design, or even theory, behind the experiment.

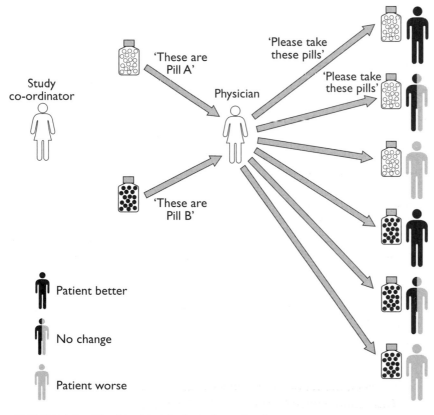

FIGURE 1.3 The 'double blind' study method

Why do we need a method like this to prove the validity of something like homeopathy? In medicine, knowledge needs to be reliable, but there is a special problem which makes the reliable study of medical treatments especially difficult – the placebo effect. People who are getting what they believe is a treatment for their complaint tend to feel better – even if there is no scientific explanation for this. To know whether a treatment really works, you need to compare it to an innocuous placebo. Only if it works better than a placebo do you believe the treatment may be responsible.

In addition, and of more significance from a scientific point of view, when collecting the evidence, the physician should *also* be unaware of which treatment is which. These are called 'double blind' studies (as in Figure 1.3) because both the patients and the physician are unaware of which treatment is which. This is the only way of preventing the physician's expectations from affecting his or her perception of which patients are getting better. 'Double blind' trials like this were first conducted in the UK in 1950. So even the scientific method has continued to evolve to help the scientist challenge their theories and assumptions.

Do you think anything similar to these 'placebo effect' problems arise in the social sciences?

Returning to homeopathy, if the experiments had not been properly blinded, the experimenters' expectations could have influenced their assessment of whether homeopathy worked. For Maddox's team, this was made significantly worse by the fact that some of the researchers were supported by homeopathic drug companies. Of course, medicinal drug trials are routinely conducted by drug companies, but in *medicine* this is not usually seen as a problem. In *science*, it seemed that Maddox's team wanted a return to the (financial) independence of the 'gentlemanly' days of the Royal Society.

The *Nature* report effectively ended homeopathy research at INSERM. Today, it is still not clear whether or not homeopathy works. Over a hundred different studies have been reported, some positive and some negative. This actually makes determining the effects of homeopathy harder rather than easier, because of **publication bias**. Because academic articles (just like newspaper articles) have to be reviewed and considered worthy of publication, there tends to be a weak bias to printing reports of experiments that found positive results rather than negative ones. Over many articles, this can quickly create the illusion of a strong trend. The same effect can arise in other publications, even the daily papers. Does publication bias contribute to a perceived feeling of widespread violent crime, belying its apparent rarity when you actually look at the figures?

Publication bias
Where evidence presented can be distorted through the procedures used to select material for publication.

Science and common sense interconnect; scientific knowledge informs common sense, although, as Table 1.1 shows, the two can be seen as having distinctive characteristics.

TABLE 1.1   'Common-sense' and scientific medical knowledge compared and contrasted

'Common-sense' medical knowledge	Scientific medical knowledge
Acquired through living in a culture and through experience	Passed on through (closed) 'learned bodies' and scientific journals
Recognized by a community	Recognized by a community
Recognizes experts	Experts are central
Often based on subjective knowledge	Claims to be based on objective knowledge
Not regarded as authoritative	Varying degrees of authority, depending on the area in science, on the person, and on the community
Informed by history, experience and science	Informed by history, experience and theory
Largely female, relatives and friends	Largely male (but changing), professionals

3   SCIENCE AND SOCIAL SCIENCE: SCIENTIFIC WAYS OF THINKING

● ●

Think back to our opening example about the diagnosis of ill health. What were the assumptions about the authority of the knowledge upon which the doctor based her diagnosis of pneumonia?

Medical science, like social science, employs its own specialist language. However, there are significant differences in the methodical approaches and the assumptions about how knowledge is produced between the social sciences and the natural sciences. Traditionally, natural science assumes that there is a measurable, material world, which can be investigated through scientific methods. Of course the sciences employ a whole range of different approaches, including activities of observation, logical reasoning and structured experimentation in which phenomena are repeated as required, with peer review of the ultimate results. There is the assumption when we receive diagnosis and treatment from our doctor that these have been based on previous experimentation, observations and on rigorous testing. Scientific method includes observation and experimentation in order to produce knowledge about the material world, which can then be used to understand, to predict and, to some extent, to gain control over the world.

3.1   How does science actually work?

Some of the popular perceptions of scientific method and the authority of scientific knowledge over other systems of knowledge derive from the creation of modern science in the West in the eighteenth century, following the Enlightenment. It has been suggested that, from this period, science replaced religion as the dominant source of knowledge (see Hall and Gieben, 1992). Empirical, rational science usurped the authoritative status of appeals to the divine and the tradition of religion. However, as the example of the Reverend Edmund Stone showed, the separation between objectivity and subjectivity is not so clear cut. Let's study this a bit more.

Edmund Stone said that he felt that it would be God's will that a natural treatment for marsh fever would grow near the marshes. What if willow bark hadn't worked? Would he have looked at other plants? Or, perhaps more seriously, would his expectation influence his judgement of whether or not willow bark really did alleviate marsh fever? It is for this reason that we expect scientists to be sceptical. Here's a joke that illustrates scepticism quite nicely.

> **Enlightenment**
> Also known as 'The Age of Reason', an intellectual movement that ran through the seventeenth and eighteenth centuries. It held that people were fundamentally rational and good, and that knowledge should be accepted through reason alone, not through tradition or religion.

BOX 1.3   **Sceptical scientists**

A philosopher, a statistician, and a biologist were travelling through Scotland when they saw a black sheep through the window of the train.

'Aha,' says the biologist, 'I see that Scottish sheep are black.'

'Hmm,' says the statistician, 'You mean that some Scottish sheep are black.'

'No,' says the philosopher, 'All we know is that there is at least one sheep in Scotland, and that at least one side of that one sheep is black!'

Of these, the philosopher is closest to being the sceptical scientist, yet it is the biologist who perhaps is closest to common sense. In some ways, science is about breaking out of common sense, about questioning *all* our assumptions. Modern Western science was based on the experimental method, as developed in the work of Francis Bacon (1561–1626), which, it was claimed, could produce reliable information about the world. The repetition of an observation or experiment with the same consequences created a conclusion that could be relied upon. This was the Baconian method of *induction,* that is, a method of arriving at a reliable conclusion by collecting data about the material world and by repeating the same experiments. If the results were always the same then you could rely on your conclusions.

In the 1930s, the social philosopher Karl Popper developed an influential challenge to this view. Popper introduced an approach to scientific method and reasoning based on scepticism and continual questioning. He argued that, no matter how many times an experiment or phenomenon was observed, one could never be certain that the same conclusion would be drawn in the future or at other times. For example, the theory 'Scottish sheep are black' is never proven true, because however many black sheep you have seen in Scotland you can never be certain that there is not a white one lurking somewhere. But we should make an epistemological virtue of this. Popper's view was that we should seek to create theories which can be disproved by evidence and testing rather than seeking to confirm what we already know. Those theories which survive testing should be tentatively accepted and regarded as closer to the truth than those we have rejected or falsified. As a consequence, the strongest theories are those that can generate the most potential for future testing rather than those that can only account for knowledge and evidence that is already known.

Popper makes the distinction between **verifying** a claim and **falsifying** it. Popper's work lies in the tradition of thought that stresses the importance of testing claims against the evidence. However, he argued that evidence could not conclusively verify or prove a claim, it could not show something to be the case under all circumstances. Instead, Popper argued that what scientists had to do was to construct experiments that would *falsify* rather than prove their hypotheses.

Verifying and falsifying
Testing theories to see whether they are true (verifying) or false (falsifying).

It is a call to scientists to adopt an open, sceptical and imaginative approach to science rather than simply a description of what they might be doing. There is a counterintuitive element to it; a whole body of research in psychology shows that people naturally tend to look for confirming evidence rather than falsifying evidence. Most scientific experimentation is concerned with proving rather than disproving hypotheses, albeit with an awareness that there cannot be absolute certainty (Rose, 1998, p.47). To return to the medical diagnosis of pneumonia that the doctor gave at the start of the chapter, most of us would not be very impressed if all our doctor could tell us was which diseases we didn't have, but that no medication could be prescribed because it would never be possible to say what we did have. Much diagnosis is speculative and most patients would prefer a possibility than the claim that nothing can ever be verified.

Popper requires scientists to be fundamentally sceptical; to be detached enough observers who are capable of rejecting theories when the evidence is against them, even when they strongly believe in these theories. In effect, it requires scientists to be suspicious of their common-sense intuitions. However, scientists can say that they accept the principle of falsification but behave differently. So, for example, they could keep the hypothesis 'Scottish sheep are black' intact by, when they find a white sheep, redefining it as a new species (not a sheep) or perhaps classifying it as an English immigrant sheep. Popper's approach to science still doesn't reduce the effect that our background has on our science. Let's look at the way a scientist's background affects the way he or she does science in a bit more detail.

To return to Edmund Stone's investigation of willow bark. How could he know that it was the willow bark that was alleviating marsh fever? There are other possible explanations for people feeling better. For example, many diseases are cyclical, or self-limiting, or may have spontaneous remission. Alternatively, people may believe that they are better just because they have been given willow bark by the learned Reverend. What Stone needed was a way to compare the effects of willow bark against something else, something which wasn't expected to help with marsh fever, something like peppermint tea, for example. If there was no difference between the effects of willow bark and peppermint tea, then willow bark is unlikely to really help with marsh fever. Only if willow bark seemed to be significantly better than peppermint tea would Stone have actually learnt something useful.

Thomas Kuhn in *The Structure of Scientific Revolutions,* argues that most of the time scientists are not even making and testing hypotheses. Their main concerns are to solve problems that have been set by earlier researchers. When scientists are doing what Kuhn called 'normal science', they are developing **paradigms** (Kuhn, 1962). Using examples from early modern Europe, Kuhn demonstrated that 'old' theories or paradigms are often replaced by new ones. There are periods of 'revolutionary science' not only because the new paradigms have superior explanatory power, but because events within society make the new paradigms more acceptable. The internal logic of science is not the only factor promoting change and development in the terrain of scientific theory; science is interconnected with social change.

Paradigms
Sets of assumptions, laws and methods that are accepted by fairly large scientific communities and set the standards for how the inquiry is conducted.

Kuhn uses a very explicit analogy between scientific and political revolutions. He argues, rather paradoxically, that 'crisis' is central to scientific progress. For Kuhn, sciences are genuinely social institutions that have a constraining influence on scientists within a field. Different sciences may proceed side by side for decades or even centuries, but occasionally a new observation or issue will arise which brings them into conflict. Because interpretation is central to science – the same results may be interpreted differently by different scientists depending on their background – it is often impossible to resolve the difference between conflicting sciences except by revolutionary upheaval. It is only because of these crisis periods of severe scientific uncertainty that the existing institutions open up to radical changes. In this interpretation, the Royal Society is not so much a cause of new science, but the remnant of a scientific revolution that happened when religious and secular theories of knowledge collided forcefully during the English Civil War in the seventeenth century.

Kuhn's argument challenges the idea of a single march of scientific progress. Scientific knowledge is produced in fits and starts, not in a single linear trajectory. Most importantly, he recognizes the links between different areas of knowledge production. Kuhn challenges the idea that although social factors can impede or hinder the advance of science they cannot affect the content of science. He focuses on scientific knowledge itself and not just the circumstances in which it is produced. After the development of Kuhn's arguments, social science could concern itself with the content of scientific knowledge as well as its context.

Kuhn's view of science as implicating the society in which it is embedded can be seen as complementing a *social constructionist* approach to knowledge. This suggests that:

> Truth is not a collection of insights floating about, parts of which are sooner or later revealed or discovered, nor does it lie deep within us, waiting to be freed. Truth is produced through discourse (based in science upon 'proper' scientific methods and investigations) and its production is involved with relations of power.
>
> (Bleier, 1984, p.195)

Science, then, is not about discovering knowledge but about producing knowledge.

3.2 Bodies of knowledge: knowledge of bodies

A social constructionist approach that links the history of science, in particular medical science, is well illustrated in the work of Michel Foucault. Foucault offers a challenge to the notion that knowledge is discovered. Rather, he argues, it is produced through the language and practices that are involved in making it meaningful. This may seem like stating the obvious, of course we cannot describe something without using words and images to do so. Foucault goes further. He claims that the body is invented or created. Think back to the example at the start of Section 2. If the physician defines the body in terms of its humours, on investigation it will be a balance of humours that is found. Foucault's approach is not just about the social and political influences on medical science. We have already suggested that medical science has specific areas of concern, for example in relation to the human body and its experience of health and, especially, of illness.

Foucault suggests that it is appropriate for medicine to concern itself with changes over time and to create new meanings. He argues that 'the body is directly involved in a political field: power relations have an immediate hold over it' (1977, p.25). It is through the intervention of the state in areas of people's lives which, hitherto, have been private, that is, excluded from public and political surveillance, that ideas about appropriate sexual behaviour and acceptable parenting, especially mothering, are produced. Categories of person are produced through medical discourses. Foucault does not deny the experience of the physical body, indeed he gives it considerable importance in his work, but he claims that conditions of the body, especially what these conditions are called and the meanings they have attached to them, are produced through medical and scientific **discourses**. For example the ways in which people experience their own bodies can be classified as healthy or unhealthy according to how medical knowledge is produced and

Discourse
A set of ideas, statements and practices that provide a way of representing a particular kind of knowledge. A discourse makes it possible to say some things but restricts what you can say.

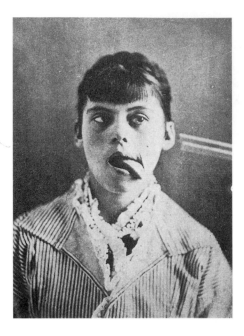

FIGURE 1.4   'Hysterical woman' photographed in 1889

applied, often through official agencies. He cites the example of the 'hysterical woman' as a recognizable classification of a type of person, which was created through nineteenth century medical discourse. This was when the figure of the 'hysterical woman' was put into discourse. Figure 1.4 shows an example of a woman classified as 'hysterical'.

You might like to think about medical conditions which were put into discourse in the late twentieth century. Sudden Infant Death Syndrome, which we look at in Section 3.4, is one example, M.E. (myalgic encephalomyelitis) is another.

Let's look at an example of how discourse produces particular forms of knowledge.

ACTIVITY 1.3

Emily Martin constructs the following quotation which combines material from two medical textbooks describing the production of human eggs and sperm.

> Of 7,000,000 egg germ cells in the female embryo most degenerate in the ovary. Of those that go on to become eggs many also degenerate. Degeneration continues through a woman's life. Oogenesis (egg production) is very wasteful. During the 40 or so years of a woman's reproductive life, 400–500 eggs will have been released ... It is still a mystery why so many eggs are formed only to die in the ovaries. Women shed only a single [egg] each month, the seminiferous tubule [in men] produces hundreds of millions of sperm each day ... How is this feat accomplished?

She goes on to describe the meeting of egg and sperm.

> The egg is transported or drifts down the fallopian tube. Sperm are small, streamlined, active and efficiently powered with strong tails and swim towards the egg. They burrow through the egg coat and penetrate the egg, although some sperm fall away after their perilous journey.
>
> (Martin, 1999, p.183–4)

- How is the production of egg and sperm described here?
- How is each described? Are their natures implicit in the choice of language?
- How does each relate to activity and passivity?
- Could they be described using different words but retaining regard for the evidence?

COMMENT

Martin uses this example to illustrate how the language of science is both gendered and culturally specific, rather than being objective, universal and neutral. Language is used that has particular connotations, for example sperm is 'produced' whereas eggs are 'shed', sperm swim actively whereas eggs 'drift'. Over-production of eggs is wasteful while an excess of sperm is an amazing feat. What seems to be biological is also cultural and differences are constructed in cultural terms. Attempts to reconstruct this material in the light of more recent developments have been equally value laden. The observation that the surface of the egg draws in the sperm, rather than the sperm plunging into the egg has been described as the egg 'trapping' or 'enveloping' the sperm which endeavours to escape. Another set of culturally specific words!

What are the implications of this for our question about how knowledge is produced? It means that the truth, or otherwise, of medical knowledge lies inside, not outside, the discourse that produces it. Claims can be refuted with reference to other claims but not to some extra discursive reality which has a stronger claim to truth than anything we can say about it. We cannot do anything other than say things about it. We cannot access it without describing it. This approach has the advantage of drawing attention to the social, economic, political and cultural processes through which claims are made and knowledge produced. Gert Brieger, a historian of medical science, argues that Foucault's stress on language and its uses in medicine as constituting the text and context of medical science has been very influential (Brieger, 1993). Not only is 'knowledge power' but, for Foucault, power and knowledge are inextricably linked (see **Allen, 2004**). It is not possible to discuss knowledge without considering the multiple points at which power is exercised in its production.

Can you think of any problems associated with this view? Is it more useful for some examples of ill health than others?

The notion of meanings produced through discourse, while emphasizing the body in Foucault's analysis, seems to marginalize people's experience of their own bodies. What about the examples of broken bones, severe physical impairment or terminal illnesses? Is it useful to see these as categories produced discursively? There is also a corporeal bottom line; an experience of pain and distress which precedes anything that could be said or done about it. Although Sudden Infant Death Syndrome is a newly classified problem, it still has a material reality in the deaths of infants, without apparent cause at this time. (This is not to say that causes may be found which could provide explanation of the phenomenon.) Foucault's analysis overemphasizes the social/cultural at the expense of the natural/body. It could be more useful to reconsider the relationship between nature and culture and look at how nature and culture interrelate, with nature and the body impacting upon culture as well as social factors shaping and producing knowledge about nature. It goes both ways. It may be that Foucault is throwing the body out with the cultural bathwater (or maybe drowning the body in discourse).

Another criticism of Foucault's more extreme social constructionist views is that they do not help us to locate the source of power in the production of knowledge. Knowledge itself produces power but are there privileged sources of knowledge? Evelyn Fox Keller's work provides an illustration of power in the production of medical and scientific knowledge, in addition, she locates the source of power. Think back to the Royal Society as an example of men being privileged over women. In its development, scientific knowledge has privileged men over women. As a result, its emphasis on objectivity and rationality has involved a value-laden association between masculinity and objectivity that is undesirable for science itself. She points firstly to the ways in which claims to the superiority of objective science ignore the values that are implicit in decisions about what to investigate, how to deploy resources and what counts as relevant or useful; secondly she describes the benefits that could accrue from embracing a more inclusive, fluid understanding of scientific knowledge.

So a social constructionist approach to knowledge sees science as historically and culturally specific. This approach has been employed in feminist critiques of claims of an objectivity which purported to be gender neutral. Fox Keller argues that modern science's claims to objectivity and the independence of the scientific observer obscures its specially gendered nature.

> Modern science ... is based on a division of emotional and intellectual labour in which objectivity, reason and 'mind' are cast as male and subjectivity, feeling and 'nature' are cast as female! Science involves a radical separation of subject and object and ultimately the domination of mind over nature. The result is a particular conception of science − one that is more suited to men than women.
>
> (Fox Keller, 1984, p.45)

An emphasis on the social and historical circumstances under which scientific investigation is carried out indicates the interrelationship between science and other sources of knowledge, and the specific values of those circumstances. As Fox Keller argues:

> Scientists' shared commitment to the possibility of reliable knowledge of nature, and to its dependence on experimental replicability and logical coherence, is an indispensable prerequisite of the effectiveness of any scientific venture ... Judgements about which phenomena are worth studying, which kinds of data are significant as well as which descriptions (or theories) of those are most adequate, satisfying, useful and even reliable, depend critically on the social, linguistic and scientific practices of those making the judgements in question.
>
> (Fox Keller, 1985)

Fox Keller is presenting a feminist critique which argues that knowledge is gendered by the social structures through which it is produced. Let's look at an example of a social structure, that of employment. Women constitute the higher proportion of employees of the National Health Service in the UK, but not in the higher echelons of the medical profession. But medicine is changing: for the first time, at the end of the twentieth century, women had equality with men in the medical profession; in the twenty-first century more women are becoming qualified doctors and more men are training as nurses. Well, actually this isn't quite true! In the tenth century in Britain, the Laws of Edgar gave women equal status with men and allowed them to becoming practising doctors. However, in 1491, this law was repealed under pressure from the (male) professional associations, including medical guilds like the College of Physicians, and women were forced to stop practising medicine.

Why was this? It was not the *practice* of medicine that was the problem – it was the *knowledge* of medicine. Women were not specifically prevented from practising medicine, but in order to practise you had to be a member of a medical guild or have received training at a university – and both of these were male institutions; as were other patriarchal institutions like organized religion.

For four hundred years, women were not permitted to practise medicine, basically because they were barred from attending universities. But this barring wasn't specific to medicine; women were excluded from other areas of public life and from higher education of any kind. Power over knowledge was used to maintain a structure in which women were systematically excluded from a male medical monopoly. One contemporary medical practice and area of what is classified as medical knowledge is obstetrics, however until the eighteenth century, this was exclusively the territory of women. It was not until men took over the management of childbirth and subsequently located it in the hospital rather than the home that it was defined as part of medical science.

Women broke the medical monopoly in two ways: first by subversion and second by opposition. Among the pioneers of the subversive approach was Mary Seacole, a skilled and experienced Jamaican 'doctress' who paid her own way to the Crimean War and treated wounded men on the battlefield. On her return she was lauded by the public and the press, and recognized by royalty. Another pioneer was James Barry, an army surgeon and political reformer with a reputation for being a 'lady killer' who, after his death, was found to have been a woman dressing as a man since entering Edinburgh University to study medicine 53 years earlier!

*Inspector General James Barry
Army Medical Department
a woman
whose sex was only discovered
after her death in 1865.*

FIGURE 1.5
Inspector General James (Miranda) Barry

FIGURE 1.6   Elizabeth Garrett

The oppositional approach was adopted by Elizabeth Garrett and Sophia Jex-Blake, who studied legally but through loopholes. They then went on to pressurize the universities, medical schools and examining bodies into accepting women. Strangely, the cases of Seacole and Barry seem to have played no part in the case for opening up medicine to women; Garrett and Jex-Blake may have had more effect because of their rather more influential social class. (Elizabeth Garrett shocked Victorian society when she added her husband's name to her own and became Elizabeth Garrett Anderson. Feminists made more of a stir recently by re-instating her original name!)

In 1876 Parliament voted that examining bodies should allow women to qualify in medicine, but it was only after the Second World War that all the top medical schools became open to women. By 1976, 20 per cent of doctors in Britain were women, and in 2000, over half those entering British medical schools were women.

TABLE 1.2   Different theorists' approaches to knowledge

	Popper	Kuhn	Foucault	Fox Keller
How do we produce knowledge?	Questions Scepticism Falsification	Paradigms	Discourses	Scientific method and practice
What is the status of knowledge?	'True science' Knowledge which survives falsification	Paradigms have status until challenged and replaced	Knowledge is power Discourses create power and knowledge together	Scientific knowledge is not objective Men have more power and status than women
How is new knowledge produced?	Through constant questioning	Social change leads to revolutionary crises	Discourses of resistance	Challenges claims to objectivity
Is this knowledge socially constructed?	Knowledge is rationally constructed by human beings	Scientific knowledge is influenced by social change and is social in content	Heavy stress on social construction There is no 'truth' outside discourse	Knowledge production is gendered and shaped by social power relations such as patriarchy

SUMMARY

- Social constructionist views challenge the idea that there is an objective truth which science can discover.

- Social constructionists point to the links between politics, science and society.

- Feminist critics point to the interconnections between power, values and the claims of medical science.

- Such critiques question the separation of objective and subjective factors and suggest that they are closely linked.

- There are limitations to the emphasis which some social constructionist views place on social processes at the expense of material, physical experience.

- Extreme social constructionist views underplay the influence of nature in the relationship between nature and culture in the production of knowledge.

- The gendered production of knowledge is illustrated by women's exclusion from medical knowledge at particular points in history.

4   WHO ARE THE EXPERTS?

We have suggested that there are different forms of knowledge and that some knowledge systems might be privileged in particular societies. While scientific knowledge can be seen as replacing religious knowledge, there is no evidence that, for example, new knowledge systems are challenging the orthodoxy of traditional medical science, especially in its application though the practice of medicine. People are seeking alternative ways of knowing about health and illness. Who are the experts now? Is there greater uncertainty about scientific forms of knowledge in the contemporary world?

At different points in history there have been different ideas about the source of authority. In the contemporary Western world, there are many competing systems of knowledge and the competition may be played out in the public arena of the media. The media play an important role in publicizing new forms of knowledge as well as in re-constructing orthodoxies. As we saw in the opening example, much of our understanding of how to define health and ill health comes from popular common-sense conceptions derived from media representations. In the following example we consider an instance in which medical certainty was

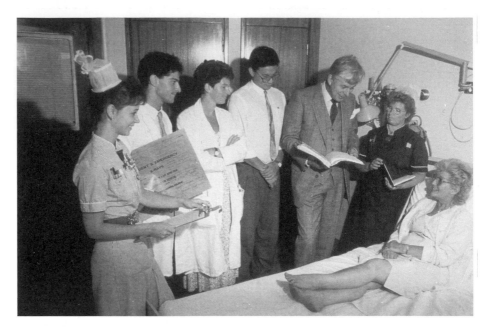

FIGURE 1.7   Expert medical authority? Teaching hospital ward round

established and then challenged with new certainties that have themselves been questioned within a very short period of time. Here we focus on competing knowledge systems. We look at a particular case study of the incidence of infant death. There is a phenomenon known as Sudden Infant Death Syndrome, SIDS, when small babies die for no apparent reason. They are not diagnosed as ill; their parents have not usually taken the infant to a medical practitioner with any particular symptoms of ill health but an apparently healthy child dies suddenly, without warning.

ACTIVITY 1.4

Read the description of case study of SIDS in Box 1.4. This is the summary of a BBC *Horizon* programme about one particular scientific investigation into the causes of the syndrome.

- What does the example of SIDS tell us about sources of knowledge in contemporary society?
- Why did the deaths of these infants become categorized as SIDS?
- What is the role of 'expert' knowledge here?
- How do social, cultural and scientific knowledge compete in this example?
- What are the cultural expectations that shape this experience?

BOX 1.4	**Sudden Infant Death Syndrome**

Sudden death: The search for the truth about cot death

Cot death kills 10 apparently healthy babies in the UK every week. They go to sleep and never wake up. Today the cause of Sudden Infant Death Syndrome (SIDS) or cot death is still a mystery. But in the 1970s a leading paediatrician, Dr Alfred Steinschneider, found a possible cause which took the US by storm: this theory was that apnoea, gaps in an infant's breathing, might kill them if they lasted too long. Several decades later, the foundation of his entire theory was shaken when it was claimed that one of his case studies was based on serial child murder.

The apnoea theory

In the mid 1960s a US couple, Waneta and Tim Hoyt, suffered a multiple tragedy. One after the other their five children died in infancy. At a time when the world was desperately looking for a cause for Sudden Infant Death Syndrome (SIDS), their case was brought to the attention of leading paediatrician Dr Alfred Steinschneider. Using his advanced baby monitoring equipment, he tracked the babies' breathing and developed an exciting new theory about SIDS. He believed there was a link between prolonged apnoea, long gaps in the babies' breathing and SIDS. He thought that constantly monitoring their breathing could save their lives. Not only that, Dr Steinschneider's observation of so many babies dying in one family led some other scientists to believe that SIDS was hereditary.

Publication

Published in 1972, Dr Steinschneider's landmark paper was devoured by the medical world, hungry for an explanation. A multi-million dollar industry sprang up manufacturing baby monitors, and extensive research into apnoea began. In Britain, Dr David Southall, from North Staffordshire Hospital decided to put Dr Steinschneider's apnoea theory to a blind test. He monitored over 9,000 babies and put the results away. Over a year later he went back to his monitoring data and traced what had happened to all the babies. He found no correlation between apnoea breathing patterns and SIDS. 'The one thing that our research really showed was that it was nonsense.' Despite Dr Southall's revelations, the baby monitoring business continued to boom and Dr Steinschneider continued his research.

The trial of Waneta Hoyt

In 1976, Dr Linda Norton, a forensic pathologist specializing in investigating violent death, began an analysis of the paper. To her, Dr Steinschneider's paper looked like the story of a multiple murder, not a medical case. 'My colleagues and I have a saying: one death in the family – SIDS; two – big question mark; three – you're dealing with multiple murder.' Dr Norton teamed up with a District Attorney and 23 years later, in an unprecedented court case, Waneta Hoyt was found guilty of murdering all five of her children. They didn't have apnoea, they had not died of SIDS, they had been smothered. Dr Steinschneider's landmark paper collapsed.

Conclusion

Waneta Hoyt died in prison in 1998. To this day, her husband believes she was innocent. She is buried with her children in an unmarked grave. Dr Steinschneider continued his research into cot death. He never answered requests from the publishing journal to retract his original paper and since the trial his research continues to be published in other journals. Although doctors are no clearer on the cause of SIDS, they are in no doubt that it is a genuine, tragic medical condition. But now they can advise a simple but effective precaution. Recent UK research found that putting a baby to sleep on its back reduces the number of cot deaths by over half.

Source: Adapted from summary of BBC TV *Horizon* programme first broadcast on 25 February 1999

COMMENT

There are different forms of knowledge in play here. Social, cultural and medical knowledges compete and sometimes complement each other. The cultural expectation that women do not harm their own children, that this is unthinkable, supports the pursuit of one branch of medical knowledge. Even though there were so many deaths in the one family, medical science sought explanations which focused on the bodies of the babies who died. Dr Norton appears to resort to folklore however in her claim, unsubstantiated by any other medical evidence here, that one death might be SIDS, two deaths pose a big question mark and three deaths equal multiple murder. This 'saying' has been repeated more recently by a leading UK expert, Professor, Sir Roy Meadow. Meadow's evidence was influential in securing the unjust imprisonment of many women, including Sally Clark, who was eventually released on appeal, for the murder of her two sons. In spite of Meadow's claims that three deaths must mean murder, the prosecution case against Trupti Patel collapsed in 2003 due to lack of evidence against her and evidence from her own family that her grandmother had experienced the sudden deaths of 5 of her own 12 babies, suggesting some possible genetic factor. Strangely, medical evidence about inherited characteristics, which have become absorbed into common sense (for example in the case of physical features and personality traits as well as inherited diseases), does not include the possibility of SIDS being a phenomenon that runs in families, although this is the subject of more recent research (Sweeney, 2003). These recent cases have resulted in conflict between different discourses, those of medical expertise and of the law, with the possibility that legal action be brought against the claimed authority of Roy Meadow. The existence of a category called SIDS made it possible for medical experts to try to fit these deaths into that category. Social, cultural and medical matters are tangled up in this scenario. This case study also illustrates the ways in which knowledge changes.

This is an instance where expert knowledge and the privileging of one version of medical science appears to have obscured information about what was happening. There is also ambiguity about the relationship between mothers and their children, and a cultural assumption that mothers protect their own infants in all circumstances. This cultural assumption may have prevented a more thorough investigation of the causes of infant death in this situation. The role of experts assumes great importance here, with the assumption that medical experts can access the truth, although medical 'truths' are challenged by legal 'truths'. There is also an indication of a competing medical perspective; scientific evidence hinted at by Dr Norton that challenges Dr Steinschneider's findings. In addition we have to think about where the new evidence about putting infants to sleep on their backs came from. This is a practice followed by large numbers of mothers. There is 'common-sense' knowledge which only becomes significant when it is classified as 'scientific research'. Scientific knowledge may still be privileged but it is contested. On occasions, the privileging of scientific knowledge may obscure other knowledge which could be more part of common sense. Nonetheless, common-sense knowledge might sometimes become scientific knowledge.

SUMMARY

- Theories and evidence for those theories are not intrinsically linked. Even when evidence for a theory is challenged, the theory itself may continue to be accepted.
- Authority strengthens a theory and may compensate for poor evidence.
- Cultural factors may play a significant role in determining which theories are accepted.
- Common-sense knowledge may be largely ignored until it is re-categorized as having a scientific basis.

5   SCIENCE AND SOCIETY

5.1   Doctors in society: medicine as a practice

There is another similarity between science and medicine; they are both **practices**. Medicine is called a practice because it is what physicians and doctors do professionally as a living – which is why we talk about doctors as medical practitioners. This structure to the medical profession, as a profession and as a practice, with moral rules bound into that practice, was first laid out in the West in the Hippocratic Oath, between the fifth and third centuries BC. Even today, most of the precepts of the Hippocratic Oath are central to Western medicine.

Practices
A practice is a professional activity, a calling or vocation, and usually binds those who follow it to a set of expectations and rules.

The Hippocratic Oath was more than a code of practice, it also formed a contract between a master and an apprentice. Master and apprentice were legal terms limited to men in a relationship defined by a contract (Kirkup and Smith Keller, 1992, p.17). Knowledge passed exclusively through this relationship. This structure made Hippocratic medical knowledge strictly a male **tradition**, distinguished from both common sense (by the fact that it was passed on within a closed apprenticeship system) and from science (by the fact that it was not systematically based on observation and experiment).

Tradition
Knowledge where authority is linked to antiquity and where its status is entirely accepted.

Superficially, this traditional side to medicine might seem to make it fundamentally different from science. Medicine can be seen as a craft and a practice, perhaps even an art, whereas science uses its theories, observations and experiments to create further knowledge about the world we live in. But science, like medicine, comprises a body of knowledge, methods, and skills that have to be learned – it is no longer enough to be born a 'gentleman' and to have attended a university. Today, scientists are professionals, paid to do research; this similarity even runs to the maleness of the tradition.

So science has adopted a social structure with a strongly traditional element bound into it. In some ways, this is very different from the days of the Royal Society, where, so long as you were a 'gentleman', you could get away with practically anything (although the role of 'gentleman' was, of course, quite strongly constraining in itself). Today, the structures of the academic publishing system and the apprenticeship model tend to reinforce areas of strong belief, making it harder to criticize or overturn beliefs. Currently, more than at any time in the past, science is a practice, with precisely the kinds of vested interests that make it hard to maintain an objective and sceptical approach to knowledge.

5.2 Science, politics and the press

Knowledge and power are interrelated. As we have seen, a group within society can be excluded from access to scientific knowledge; one group may exert power to exclude another. But scientific knowledge and debate is not always constrained to the closed pages of academic journals. Scientific evidence is routinely used to back up, or to attack, common-sense views, government policies and other matters of public debate. Again, health is an excellent way of illustrating these issues, as not only is health strongly linked to economic and political issues, it is controversial enough to provide good fuel for public debate (see **Smith and Goldblatt, 2004**).

An obvious example of a health question that raises political and economic issues as well as medical and scientific ones is what to do about smoking. Governments gain substantial revenues from taxes on cigarettes, which they then have to spend on providing health care for those whom smoking affects.

Civil liberties are at stake. How is someone's 'right to smoke' balanced by the rights of others who have the right not to inhale other people's cigarette smoke in public places? To help you decide, you need more evidence; you need to know scientifically *and* medically what effect smoking has. This evidence should then open up public debate on the matter, and help decide how the political and economic issues interact with the medical and scientific ones.

At least, that's the theory. How does it work in practice? Let's look at a slightly different – and slightly less contentious example. Heart diseases and strokes are among the biggest killers in the UK, but what actually causes them?

ACTIVITY 1.5

What do you think might be the most significant influences on the mortality rates for heart diseases and strokes? See if you can rank the following factors in order of their significance:

- inherited risk 4
- diet 1
- stress 3
- smoking 2
- latitude 8
- environmental temperature 7
- average rainfall 9
- wealth 6
- social class 5

COMMENT

The evidence might surprise you. The biggest risk factors are inherited risk, smoking, environmental temperature and wealth. Environmental temperature, average rainfall and socio-economic factors, such as wealth and class, account for more than 40 per cent of the differences between similar towns. Temperature is very significant; for a 1°C difference in environmental temperature, there can be as much as 7 per cent difference in the death rates from stroke and heart disease. Social class has limited effect, but financial deprivation is strongly associated with the mortality rate.

Some of these influences are biological. They can be addressed through medicine and science. Others are definitely social and addressing these requires other forms of action. This can vary from enabling doctors to prescribe loft insulation to the more politically controversial ending of 'fuel poverty'.

This evidence was discussed in the *British Medical Journal*, the official journal of the British Medical Association. The evidence was used to argue that charging VAT on fuel, which had recently been adopted as a government policy, from a health perspective, would be counterproductive. The moral argument (that charging VAT on fuel was 'unfair' and would widen the gap between rich and poor) was backed by a scientific argument that overcoming 'fuel poverty' and improving heating and insulation would lead to better health, less cost to government social services, and increased spending in local economies.

The following editorial appeared in the *British Medical Journal*:

DOCTORS FOUGHT NUCLEAR WEAPONS, NOW THEY CAN FIGHT POVERTY

This week the BMJ publishes its fourth issue in two years that has clustered papers on inequalities in health. Why all the fuss?

Some suggest that it's because the BMJ is politically motivated. If that means the BMJ wants action on a major threat to health, it's true. We would like all political parties in all countries to pay attention to inequalities in health. Many are reluctant to do so. They are more concerned to cut taxes and so win the votes of what the economist J. K. Galbraith calls the comfortable majority.

(*British Medical Journal*, 22 February 1997)

So why is medicine seen as separate from politics and economics? Is the type of knowledge it uses and generates very different? It seems rather strange to *attack* a scientific journal as being politically motivated. Maybe this is recognizing the connection between science and politics. This criticism, which is basically saying that medical scientists aren't being purely passive observers of medical phenomena, is hardly surprising. As we have seen, no scientist is a purely passive observer. All scientists are motivated by something, so why should political motivation be seen as a special issue?

This criticism seems to imply that all knowledge should be compartmentalized in pure categories. Medical knowledge should address medicine and only medicine; political knowledge should address only politics, physical knowledge only physics, and so on. However, not only is this not how people – even scientists – work in practice, it never was like this in medicine. Remember the Greek physicians mentioned in Section 2 who needed to know logic, physics and ethics, as well as medicine. In the days of the Royal Society, almost everything fell into the category of 'natural philosophy', whether it was medical science, astrology, or Newton's newfangled laws of motion.

No, the issue lies deeper than that. Bodies of knowledge, such as medicine and politics, through their community structures, and the apprenticeship and peer review systems that maintain these communities, behave as social institutions in their own right. They are structures that constrain and shape the knowledge of the agents that work within them. Unfortunately, the world is a much more tangled place than this image reflects and, as we have seen, medical knowledge has political implications, and *vice versa*. Compartmentalization will never truly happen, but with the scientific structures that are in place today, a bias towards compartmentalization and competition between bodies of knowledge seems to be inevitable.

SUMMARY

- Medical and scientific knowledge are – even today – largely transmitted through a traditional apprenticeship system.

- Restricting scientific and medical knowledge can construct self-perpetuating and self-maintaining exclusive communities with authority and power over others.

- Decisions about the access to and use of scientific and medical knowledge tend to be based on factors external to science and medicine, and are often made by dominant political groups.

6 CONCLUSION

At this point, let us return to opening question: what counts as knowledge?

Knowledge comes in several different forms, which are nonetheless interrelated. You can have common-sense and scientific knowledge. Medical science is characterized by competing and complementary knowledges. They differ at several points: how the knowledge is constructed, how it is transmitted, and the legitimacy and authority that is placed upon it by scientific and other institutions. The same knowledge (for example, the maxim 'like cures like') can be both common-sense and scientific knowledge, depending on who says it and the evidence they present in its favour. Common-sense knowledge can become scientific knowledge if it can be proven and if an authoritative community accepts that proof.

Scientific knowledge also illuminates the main themes of this book. We have seen how issues like uncertainty and even crisis are central to the development of science. Knowledge in science develops through periods of stability interspersed with revolutions. And for most of science, a certain amount of diversity is not a problem – the single forum of the Royal Society accepted everything from Newton's laws of motion to Stone's report on the effect of willow bark on fever. Indeed, if the history of medical knowledge tells us anything, it is that a lack of diversity is more likely to lead to science becoming a series of revolutions. Today, with the acceptance of complementary rather than alternative medicine, there is a diversity of systems of medical knowledge available.

There are reflections of the tension between individual agency and social structures in knowledge too – knowledge of all kinds, not just in science. The development of science depends both on small-scale structures like the apprenticeship system and on larger-scale structures like the British Medical Association. Structures such as these are needed to direct the transmission of knowledge – and in the case of science, to provide the kind of authority on which it depends. However, these structures can constrain individual interpretation and use of knowledge in ways which lead to precisely the kind of crises that modify these same structures. Individual and collective agency can challenge and transform these structures; for example women's actions have led to the reconstruction of patriarchal organizations and social structures.

If there is one moral from this chapter, it is that scientific knowledge is not opposed to social science or to common-sense knowledge, but is interrelated. Science began as a new method to rationalize and prove knowledge – much of it common-sense knowledge – with an apparent objectivity. However, scientists are members of a society, and the society in which they live shapes and constrains the scientific knowledge they produce. Science is not separate from society, but a part of it.

SUMMARY

- There are whole ranges of different systems of knowledge that provide information about sickness and ill health.

- Knowledge in medical science is produced in particular circumstances at particular times; it is historically specific.

- Such knowledge of medical science is characterized by specialized language which defines and delimits what is included and what is excluded.

- New ideas and language in medical science are created in response to what has gone before; existing discourses are challenged by new systems of knowledge.

- In the contemporary UK there are different sets of knowledge, both competing and complementary, upon which we draw in defining illness.

- There are challenges to the traditional authority and expertise of medical science (and other systems of scientific knowledge). This proliferation of different ideas can create uncertainty as well as diversity.

REFERENCES

Allen, J. (2004) 'Power: its institutional gender and disguises' in Fergusson, R. and Hughes, G. (eds) *Ordering Lives: Family, Work and Welfare* (2nd edn), London, Routledge/The Open University.

Bleir, B. (1984) *Social Science and Gender: a Critique of Biology and its Theories on Women*, Oxford, Pergamon Press.

Brieger, G. (1993) 'The historiography of medicine' in Bynum, W.G. and Porter, R. (eds) *Companion Encyclopaedia of the History of Medicine*, London, Routledge, pp.24–44.

Chalmers, A. F. (1998) *What is This Thing Called Science?* (3rd edn), Buckingham, Open University Press.

Foucault, M. (1977) *History of Sexuality, Vol.1*, Harmondsworth, Penguin.

Fox Keller, E. (1984) Untitled article in *Technology Review*, vol.87, no.8, pp.45–7.

Fox Keller, E. (1985) *Reflections on Gender and Science*, New Haven, Yale University Press.

Haines, A. and Smith, R. (1997) 'Working together to reduce poverty's damage', *British Medical Journal*, vol.314, no.22, p.529.

Hall, S. and Gieben, B. (1992) *Formation of Modernity*, Cambridge, Polity.

Harding, S. (1991) *Whose Science, Whose Knowledge?*, Buckingham, Open University Press.

Kirkup, G. and Smith Keller, L. (eds) (1992) *Inventing Women*, Cambridge, Polity.

Kuhn, T. S. (1962) *The Structure of Scientific Revolution,* Chicago, University of Chicago Press.

Maddox, J., Randi, J. and Stewart, W.W. (1988) '"High-dilution" experiments a delusion', *Nature*, vol.334, no.28, July, pp.287–90.

Martin, E. (1999) 'The egg and the sperm: How science has constructed a romance based on stereotypical male/female roles' in Price, J. and Shildrick, M. (eds) *Feminist Theory and the Body*, Edinburgh, Edinburgh University Press, pp.179–89.

Nettleton, S. (1995) *The Sociology of Health and Illness,* Cambridge, Polity.

New Scientist (1997) 'Feedback', vol.155, no.2098, 6 September 1997, p.96.

Oakley, A. (2000) *Experiments in Knowing: Gender and Method in the Social Sciences*, Cambridge, Polity.

Porter, R. (1997) *The Greatest Benefit to Mankind: A Medical History of Humanity from Antiquity to the Present,* London, HarperCollins.

Rose, S. (1998) *Lifelines*, Harmondsworth, Penguin.

Schiff, M. (1997) *The Memory of Water: Homoeopathy and the Battle of Ideas in the New Science*, London, Thorsons.

Smith, B. and Goldblatt, D. (2004) 'Whose health is it anyway?' in Hinchliffe, S. and Woodward, K. (eds) *The Natural and the Social: Uncertainty, Risk, Change* (2nd edn), London, Routledge/The Open University.

Sweeney, J. (2003) 'Cot deaths and justice' in *The Observer,* London, 15 June, p.27.

FURTHER READING

Roy Porter's *The Greatest Benefit to Mankind* (1997) provides a fascinating and comprehensive coverage of the growth of Western medicine and the construction of medical knowledge.

Steven Rose's *Lifelines* (1988) offers a interesting critique of the development of scientific knowledge and further analysis of some of the theories presented here.

Sandra Harding's *Whose Science, Whose Knowledge?* (1991) provides a feminist critique of the production of scientific knowledge and reviews feminist theories.

Anne Oakley's *Experiments in Knowing* (2000) offers useful coverage of social sciences methodologies, both quantitative and quantitative, with a particular focus on quantitative methods within the context of a gendered approach to the history of social sciences (also useful for Chapter 2).

Knowing and believing: religious knowledge

Ken Thompson and Kath Woodward

Contents

1   INTRODUCTION

How do we know? Chapter 1 explored a particular kind of knowledge and used the example of medical science to examine questions about what we mean by knowledge and especially how knowledge is socially constructed. In this chapter we move to a different kind of knowledge and to a different question. Here our concern is not so much with 'What do we know?', as it was in the first chapter, but with '*How do we know?*' In order to look at how social scientists investigate the production of knowledge we are going to focus on religious knowledge – a category of knowledge which, it could be argued, has, in parts of the world, been usurped and overtaken by scientific knowledge, especially that of the natural sciences. Our concern is not with the truth or falsity of religious knowledge but with how we find out about the social meanings that are attached to religion. Has religious knowledge become less important in contemporary society than at earlier times? How do we know?

1.1   How do we know about religion?

FIGURE 2.1   Front cover of *Newsweek*, 12 July 1999

The front cover of *Newsweek*, the international news magazine for 12 July 1999, had the large headline, 'Is God dead?', followed by the comment, 'In Western Europe, it sure can look that way' (see Figure 2.1).

What does this headline mean? The image is clearly designed to shock. The question is not about God but about people, and in particular about an alleged decline in religious worship and practice. What is addressed in this question, and in the accompanying articles in the magazine, is religious observance in Western Europe. Religion as a form of knowledge, which in the past had certainty and authority, is seen as much reduced; the headline even suggests that it is finished. Not only might religious knowledge have been surpassed by that of science as a source of authority, but religion might be seen to have *no* authority in the contemporary world. The story on the inside pages which accompanies the front cover picture makes for sober reading. It includes some figures which it is claimed record church attendance in recent years. The claim made in the shocking headline is apparently supported by empirical evidence (see Figure 2.2).

Open the doors – and where are the people?

Even in such Roman Catholic bastions as Italy and Ireland, where formal religious observance is an integral part of daily life, church membership and attendance have fallen.

Respondents attending church regularly

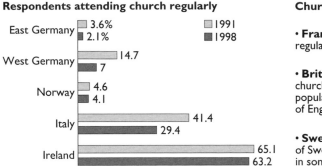

Churchgoing in Europe

• **France** Only 3–4% of Parisians regularly attended church in 1998.

• **Britain** 89% didn't attend church regularly in 1995; 99% of the population didn't attend the Church of England in 1999.

• **Sweden** 85% belong to the Church of Sweden, but less than 50% believe in some kind of afterlife.

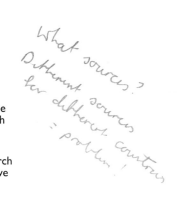

FIGURE 2.2

Sources: *Newsweek*, 12 July 1999, p.52. Data: 1991/98 comparative country data from International Social Survey Program; National Secular Society; Office of the Archbishop of Paris

ACTIVITY 2.1

What do these figures tell us? Are they comparable and reliable?

C O M M E N T

We cannot check the *Newsweek* figures for accuracy, as we do not have access to all their sources of information. However, it is very important to look carefully at the sources of the statistics, especially when there is a mixture of sources. In this case, the varied nature of the sources might raise concerns about the comparability and reliability of the figures.

The statistics for regular church attendance in different European countries in 1998 appear to show continuing decline since 1991, down to as low as 2.1 per cent in East Germany and 4.1 per cent in Norway. In Britain, the attendance figure for 1995 was 11 per cent (i.e. 100 per cent minus the 89 per cent who didn't attend church regularly), whilst in such Roman Catholic bastions as Italy and Ireland it was 29.4 per cent and 63.2 per cent respectively in 1998 (the Irish figure is probably an overestimate). The fact that these figures are drawn from very different sources is a matter of some concern, especially as we do not know the questions asked or methods used. The figures under the heading 'Churchgoing in Europe' appear to have been drawn from sources as diverse as the National Secular Society and the Office of the Archbishop of Paris. We need to ask questions about the evidence which is used to support the claim that religion is in decline, but also to question what sort of evidence might be useful. What might be a more reliable single source, the UK census 2001, revealed that 71.7 per cent of people in England and Wales consider themselves to be Christian, although church attendance rates remained at 11 per cent in 2001.

If the measure of religious belief were church attendance, then this evidence indicates a decline, although this is not the only indicator, as we argue in this chapter.

In one of the accompanying articles in the same edition of *Newsweek*, Karen Armstrong began with a quotation from the philosopher Friedrich Nietzsche, prophet of a post-religious world, who in 1882 proclaimed that God was dead. However, Armstrong then went on to say that, in one sense, the twentieth century has proved Nietzsche wrong:

> Since the 1970s, religion has once again become a factor in public life in a way that would have once seemed inconceivable. The Iranian revolution was succeeded by an eruption of Islamist revivalist movements in the Middle East. At about the same time the Moral Majority and the new Christian right tried to bring God back into public life in the United States, whilst ultra-orthodox Jews and radical Zionists have done the same in Israel. Now no government can safely ignore religion. The assassinations of Anwar Sadat in Egypt and of Yitzhak Rabin in Israel are sober reminders of the lethal danger of some forms of modern faith.
>
> (Armstrong, 1999, p.56)

On the one hand it seems that religious observance might be on the decline, especially in Europe, while on the other there appear to be explosions of religion in public life across the globe which suggest that religion is literally a force to be reckoned with. (The differences within Europe and between Europe and other areas are discussed by Davie, 2000.) This chapter explores the role of religion in the contemporary world, but focuses on the UK in the post-war period. This may need to be balanced against the different developments in other parts of the world, such as the United States, Iran and Latin America, but our concern here is mainly with the UK.

Many of the explosions of private faith into the public sphere are spurred by the challenges to traditional religious certainties and by a fear that modernization threatens to kill off religious thinking and activity. New knowledges challenge the authority of traditional religious knowledge. There are several major causes of this sense of threat to religion. The first is the **secularization** of social functions that were once performed by organized religion, such as welfare and education, which have largely been taken over by the state. The second is the decline in involvement in organized religion as other lifestyle and leisure activities have successfully competed for people's time and attention. The third is the relative decline in the authority of religious thinking compared with other forms of thought, especially science. It is this issue of what is happening to religion as a form of knowledge that will be our main focus, and in particular the claim that religious knowledge has lost impact and importance. The debate about the decline of religion has come to be known as the **secularization thesis**. In this chapter we are going to look at how we find out about knowledge using the example of religious knowledge and concentrating particularly on the apparent decline in religion as illustrated by the secularization debate.

Secularization
A term used to describe the apparent process of decline of religious belief and worship in contemporary society.

Secularization thesis
The debate in social science about the phenomenon of secularization. An argument and claim that the process of secularization is taking place, which is contested by some social scientists.

1.2 The status of religious knowledge

Religious knowledge can be seen as a particular kind of knowledge: one based on beliefs in truths revealed, rather than discovered through empirical investigation or subject to critical reason and rational thought process.

The success of scientific thinking, especially as associated with the natural sciences in the modern world, might seem to render other ways to 'truth' redundant, especially if religion is thought of as a rival system of thought in competition with science to explain the same phenomena. It was this idea of competition between science and religion to explain physical events that sparked off public controversy in the nineteenth century, as in the public debates between scientists and bishops about the theory of evolution. In the 1860 debate on evolution held at Oxford, in which the scientist T.H. Huxley was opposed by the Bishop of Oxford, Samuel Wilberforce, Huxley is alleged to have said that he 'would rather be descended from an ape than a bishop' (he subsequently denied saying it!). However, not all scientists considered that belief in evolution and in God were incompatible, or that the book of *Genesis* was intended by its author as an empirically scientific description of the origins of creatures. Charles Darwin himself, at the time of publication of his *Origin of the Species* in 1859, still believed in God, although not as a Christian. But many non-scientists, who had never considered these questions before, were disturbed by the popular accounts they read in the newspapers and believed that science had disproved religion. In the twenty-first century, religion has usually sought to avoid being seen as in competition with science.

As we saw in the previous chapter, science gradually took over from religion as the most authoritative form of knowledge in modern society. However, as was noted, the authority of science, especially the natural sciences, rests to some extent on what people believe about it – both within the community of scientists and within the larger community of society. There is also a considerable diversity of scientific knowledge. For example, as we saw in Chapter 1, medical science is contested from within, as well as by alternative and complementary health care practices. Within the scientific community there are differences of opinion about how scientific knowledge relates to religious knowledge, just as there are differences within society at large. They may be seen as in conflict (e.g. that between the theory of evolution and a literal belief in the biblical account of creation in six days). Others see them as independent modes of thought (e.g. the view that science asks 'How?', whereas religion asks 'Why?'). Knowledge in the natural sciences is produced in different ways from religious knowledge which is seen to be revealed through spiritual experience or a sacred text; it is claimed to be revelatory rather than the outcome of empirical investigation or scientific rational deduction. Sometimes scientific and religious knowledge may be in dialogue, with a recognition of overlapping interests (e.g. concerning the history of the universe or the nature of the human person). Occasionally there is an attempt at integration. For example, Teilhard de Chardin, a Jesuit priest and palaeontologist, attracted a great deal of interest in the 1950s by weaving together biological and spiritual evolution in a theory of 'cosmogenesis', which was an amalgam of science, theology and poetry. On the whole, however, the decline or persistence of religious belief in society probably has less to do with the authority of science than it has to do with the extent to which science and other specialized forms of knowledge (including medicine) succeed or fail in answering certain needs which religion does address.

Like natural scientists, social scientists have taken various stances on the relation between their form of knowledge and religious knowledge. Some of the early contributors to the development of social science saw their task as being to criticize religion on the grounds that it was opposed to science and progress. Karl Marx, in the nineteenth century, regarded it as a 'false consciousness' and as 'the opium of the people', insisting that: 'The abolition of religion as the *illusory* happiness of the people is required for their *real* happiness.'(Marx, 1844/undated, p.42). His French contemporary and the founder of sociology, Auguste Comte, pronounced that human thought passed through three stages – theological, metaphysical and then scientific ('positive') – which supposedly paralleled the individual's intellectual development from childhood through adolescence and then adulthood (Comte, 1842–53; Thompson, 1976).

Subsequently, as we shall see, most social scientists have adopted a more neutral stance, concentrating on mapping out some of the social functions that religion seems to serve for different groups, or seeking to interpret how religious knowledge might make otherwise senseless things meaningful. These are questions completely separate from that of the truth or falsity of religious beliefs. Social scientists are not interested in the truth or falsity of religious prescriptions, nor even in whether or not God – or gods – exist. They are more concerned with how religion works, how religious knowledge is produced and its social impact. In this chapter we will be looking at how social scientists can find out about how religious knowledge works. How do we know about religion's impact and about how religious knowledge fulfils people's needs?

According to many social scientists, it is the inability of science to give moral prescriptions, or to offer psychological and emotional comfort, that explains the presence and continuing influence of non-scientific knowledge in modern society. It is here that religion still plays a part, often in combination with other ways of thinking, including political ideologies such as nationalism or ethnic unity – as in the former Yugoslavia and Northern Ireland. Some social scientists find a religious dimension in new moral causes, such as ecology and animal rights and in the upsurge of various New Age and occult beliefs. Some of the new social movements of the 1960s and 1970s in Europe and in the USA crossed the boundaries between politics, religion and science. For example, the women's movement in different forms challenged patriarchy and its orthodoxies in traditional politics, medicine and health care, and in the established church and in organized religions. Such new social movements combined moral, political and scientific dimensions in movements organized around collective action.

Questions of identity (see **Woodward, 2004**) and the relation of human beings to their past (tradition) and future (e.g. the ideal society, or the use of earth's resources), are subjects to which non-scientific ways of thinking continue to make a contribution. In contrast to some versions of the secularization theory, which we will discuss later, the perspective taken in this chapter does not maintain that the development of modern societies entails a process in which non-scientific knowledge inevitably becomes less and less important. It is more interested in what this knowledge does for people – in the way of giving meaning, a sense of continuity and order to events, and comfort – than in whether or not it is true.

We are going to use the claim that religion might be in decline to investigate how social scientists explore the production of knowledge. *How can social scientists investigate religious knowledge and its relevance in the contemporary UK?* In order to explore this big question, the chapter is framed around three questions:

- What is religious knowledge and how do we know about it?
- What is the status of religion in the contemporary UK; is it subject to more uncertainty than in the past?
- If there are uncertainties, do changes in the practice of religion offer more opportunities for diverse forms of spiritual expression?

2 WHAT IS RELIGIOUS KNOWLEDGE?

● ●

ACTIVITY 2.2

Think about what you associate with religion. What words, places and practices mark religion in the society in which you live? How is religious knowledge differentiated from other sets of knowledge – from natural science for example?

COMMENT

The most likely associations would be those which involve belief, spirituality, special rituals and places which may be set apart from everyday life and may be worthy of particular respect. For many believers across the globe, religious belief is what guides them in every aspect of their lives; it cannot be distinguished from everyday life. Within some faiths there can be no separation between religion and everyday practices. However religion does suggest some appeal to a higher authority and a dimension beyond that which is routine. There may be different degrees of formality, but religion may suggest something set apart, or special, with its own words and practices. The language of religion embraces spiritual aspects of experience based on faith and belief rather than observable, empirical testing. Religious knowledge is sanctified by appeal to a higher authority and to tradition; it is not subject to experimental testing and critical enquiry like science. The French sociologist Emile Durkheim defined religion in terms of a distinction between the **sacred** and the **profane**. The sacred includes symbols and objects treated apart from routine aspects of life, which are the realms of the profane. Religious knowledge is produced through particular language, rituals and practices which are, on the whole, very different from those employed by science. Scientific knowledge is seen as quantifiable, rational and subject to empirical testing, whereas religion deals with the immeasurable, the ineffable, and the divine.

Sacred
Dimension of human experience relating to what is set apart and separate from the everyday.

Profane
The routine and ordinary practices of everyday human life.

Substantive definition
A substantive definition of religion concerns its content.

Functional definition
A functional definition of religion focuses on the purpose served by religion in society.

Discussion of religion has to begin with a definition of the term. There are two main types of definition: **substantive** (or exclusive) and **functional** (or inclusive). A substantive definition of religion is concerned with stating what it *is*, such as beliefs and practices relating to the supernatural, and so excludes anything that does not clearly have that reference. A *functional* definition, on the other hand, is concerned with what religion *does* – such as answering otherwise unanswerable questions (Is there life after death? What is the meaning of life?), or binding people together through a shared fundamental commitment – and this definition would include anything that serves such a function. For example, the German sociologist of religion,

Max Weber, implicitly adopted a substantive definition. He was concerned with the content of particular religions, especially with their ethical content. In his most famous work, *The Protestant Ethic and the Spirit of Capitalism* (Weber, 1904/1930), he focused his attention on the content of certain Calvinist religious beliefs, but also included their ethical implications for individuals' economic behaviour, and the role played by this economic behaviour in the development of seventeenth-century capitalism.

His contemporary, Emile Durkheim, in *The Elementary Forms of the Religious Life*, adopted a mainly functionalist definition of religion but also included a substantive element that he called the 'sacred' as distinct from the 'profane' (everything else): 'A religion is a unified system of beliefs and practices relative to sacred things, that is to say, things set apart and forbidden – beliefs and practices which unite into one single moral community called a church, all those who adhere to them' (Durkheim, 1912/1965, p.21) The emphasis here is on religion's functional quality of binding those people together who share a commitment to the same sacred symbol, and who are then united in a 'moral community'. It is the moral bonding that is significant, not the particular object of devotion (anything could become a sacred symbol – ranging from a sacred bird as a totem for an Australian aboriginal clan, to the bread and wine as the body and blood of Christ in the Christian Church). Particular rituals provide occasions when people come together to experience this sense of community.

Which sorts of rituals do you associate with particular religious belief systems? What do you think are the purposes of these rituals? Can you think of examples of situations where religious rituals combine with those of other institutions?

Attendance at a place of worship, as well as appropriate religious observances which take place in the home, are all rituals which bring people together in religious communities. There are also examples of religious rituals which are used to give particular weight to secular occasions, such as memorial services after tragedies and disasters. The fact that the English monarch as Head of the State is also head of the established Church of England further forges links between religious and political rituals in England.

2.1   Two different traditional approaches

The choice of a substantive or functional definition of religion and religious knowledge has an effect on how we view what is happening to it in modern society. Those who adopt an exclusive or substantive definition, with an emphasis on the supernatural content of religion, are likely to talk about religion declining as modern society becomes 'demystified' or 'disenchanted'. This was Weber's view of the rationalization process of modernization, in which rational calculation pushed out more traditional modes of thought based on spiritual values or sanctified custom. Durkheim, by contrast, viewed religion as serving essential social functions that would continue, even if the symbols changed:

> Thus there is something eternal in religion which is destined to survive all the particular symbols in which religious thought has successively enveloped itself. There can be no society which does not feel the need of upholding and reaffirming at regular intervals the collective sentiments and the collective ideas which make its unity and its personality.
>
> (Durkheim, 1912/1965, p.475)

When social scientists have adopted a functional definition of religion they have tended to concentrate their attention on the changing forms of religion, or on belief systems that seem to serve the same social functions as religion. In the latter case they may include such diverse phenomena as nationalism or a revolutionary cause, in which people are bound together and share a common identity by virtue of their devotion to something held sacred. As Durkheim pointed out, even the French Revolution of 1789, which had as one of its objectives the overthrow of religion, soon assumed many of the aspects of a religious revolution, with sacred symbols and moral obligations. The American sociologist, Robert Bellah, has written about his own country as having evolved a 'civil religion', in addition to the many formal religious groups, with rituals and ceremonies such as swearing allegiance to the American flag in schools, and celebrations of Memorial Day, Thanksgiving, Martin Luther King Day, and so on (Bellah, 1970). The equivalent in Britain would be the traditions (some of recent invention) surrounding the Royal Family and associated ceremonies, such as the coronation, jubilees, royal weddings, and services of remembrance, although the sacred aura may have been lessened by the marital problems of the royals, only partly offset by the remarkable elevation of the late Princess Diana to an almost saintly status.

According to this functionalist perspective, it is society that needs these religious functions to be served in some form or other. Religion does not only satisfy the needs of individuals, it has a social purpose. From the functionalist perspective, religion is universal because it performs an essential integrative function for society.

As a leading British sociologist of religion, Grace Davie, points out, there are close links between definitions of religion and the ongoing debate about whether religion is inevitably declining in modern society – the 'secularization thesis':

> Those who see religion primarily in substantive terms are more likely to argue that western society is becoming increasingly secular, for what they perceive as religion is diminishing in a way that can be convincingly measured (for example in the marked decline in regular churchgoing in almost all western European countries in the post-war period) ... . Those who see religion in functional terms, however, will be less convinced, for they will want to include within the definition a set of phenomena that at the very least meet the Durkheimian description of the sacred. These are phenomena which show considerable persistence even in contemporary societies.
>
> (Davie, 1999, p.284)

2.1.1 Recent developments

A somewhat different emphasis from the functionalism that stresses society's needs is that which starts with the needs of the individual to have answers to questions about the meaning of things that cannot be answered other than in religious terms. Here the question is not so much what can religion do for society, but, rather, why do people hold religious beliefs, why do we believe? This is sometimes referred to as the **phenomenological** perspective on religion. Phenomenologists begin from the assumption that human individuals need to see the world as a meaningful, ordered and coherent place. Human existence constantly throws up apparently inexplicable challenges, such as suffering, misery and 'bad luck'; non-scientific knowledge and beliefs are necessary to give meaning to such otherwise senseless events. The latter provide explanations which help us to cope and they may also offer ways of behaving which allow us to represent and express our desire for meaning and order. For example, ritual can be seen as a kind of language, allowing its participants to express their feelings about the world symbolically – articulating through action the way they would like the world to be. The task of the social scientist, from this perspective, is to interpret the symbol system and the way it works for participants.

In the phenomenological perspective, religion is universal because it fulfils the human need to make otherwise senseless things meaningful. This phenomenological approach gained its most forceful advocacy in the 1970s through the work of Peter Berger. In his book, *The Social Reality of Religion* (1969) – American title *The Sacred Canopy* (1967) – Berger argued that religion provides a shield or 'sacred canopy' against meaninglessness. He acknowledged that there are other meaning systems, including science, but religion is distinguished by the fact that it covers all phenomena (the cosmos) and also tells us how to behave towards them. Religion may be used to explain natural phenomena but it also, importantly, provides moral guidelines and meanings which other sorts of knowledge, like the natural sciences, do not. Its sheltering quality is particularly important in marginal situations in the lives of individuals, where taken-for-granted definitions of reality are called into question, such as when the sense of identity is disturbed. The marginal situation *par excellence* is death. It is in witnessing the death of others (especially of significant others), and in anticipating their own death, that individuals are led to question what Berger called 'the *ad hoc* cognitive and normative operating procedures' of their normal life in society. Such marginal situations reveal the innate precariousness of the meaningful order (nomos) on which everyday social life depends and threaten the individual with meaninglessness (anomie). Religion buttresses the meaningful order (nomos) by grounding it in a sacred cosmos. 'Put differently', Berger says, 'religion is the audacious attempt to conceive of the entire universe as being humanly significant' (Berger, 1967, p.28).

Phenomenology
The development in sociology of a philosophical approach which focuses on people's consciousness of their experiences and how they interpret the world; the meaning it has for them.

SUMMARY

- Religion can be seen as concerning what is set apart as sacred, marked off from the profane.
- Substantive and functionalist definitions of religion offer contrasting approaches.
- Substantive approaches, which focus on content, such as those based on Weber's views, are more likely to stress the decline of religion in modern society.
- Functionalist approaches emphasis the purpose which is served by religion; the content and form may change, but religion can still unite people and provide a sense of belonging to a community.
- Phenomenological approaches focus on the meanings which religion has for individuals.

2.2 Methods: finding out

In the Introduction to this chapter, we indicated that one of the ways in which social scientists attempt to investigate the initial question about secularization might be to produce evidence of church attendance. There are different methods associated with gathering evidence with which to support or refute the claims which social scientists make. The methods chosen are also based on different assumptions about what constitutes knowledge and the relationship between that knowledge and the world which it purports to describe and ultimately explain.

2.2.1 How do we know? Positivist and interpretative approaches

Religious knowledge may present a particularly problematic area of enquiry for the social scientist. If religion is about personal belief, it is difficult to investigate people's subjective experience and the meanings which they attach to that experience. On the other hand, questionnaires may offer one way of finding out about people's participation in religion. We can record membership of religious organizations and observe behaviour. The next stage would be to ascertain some connections between the behaviour and practices of individuals or groups and and more general trends or laws. Such an approach has been categorized as **positivist**.

Positivist
Approaches based on observation which claim to exclude subjective understandings.

Positivism is based on the assumption that we can only learn about the world and about people and social relations through observation of what people do. Positivism entails a view of the world in line with modern natural sciences and which, accordingly, might appear to devalue religion and pre-scientific or superstitions forms of thought. This certainly characterized positivism in the nineteenth century.

Positivism has involved an approach which measures and quantifies human behaviour and draws conclusions from this in order to establish structural explanations. It has stressed the quantifiable aspects of human experience rather than the meanings which people might attach to their own actions, including the intentions and the motives they may have for acting as they do. Surveys may record opinions but they tend not to interrogate the reasons people have for holding them. Positivism has been criticized by some social scientists as too limiting, on the grounds that human subjects are different from objects in the natural world and cannot be treated in the same way. There is always an element of human intentionality to take into account, whether of the social scientist who carries out the investigation, or of the respondent or person being observed. However, this is not to say that quantifiable evidence, especially statistical data, is not a vital component in providing support or rebuttal for the claims made in the social sciences. Although positivism is not a view espoused by many contemporary social scientists, quantitative evidence is very important and, as we have already seen, the empirical evidence can provide a very useful starting point for our study of religion.

Positivism has been challenged by more **interpretative** approaches which seek to interpret human action and focus on understanding the meanings which people give to their own action. This shifts the emphasis from observation to understanding and allows for more *agency*, and it challenges the more restrictive imposition of categories from outside. Interpretative approaches involve a view of areas of enquiry in the social sciences as different from the natural sciences, and reject positivists' claim that the physical sciences should be the model for all investigations.

Interpretative
Approaches which include understanding of meanings which people give to their actions.

Such views challenge the positivist claim that evidence should be used to make causal links and establish general laws. Social science investigation may involve making connections and correlations but there can be a multiplicity of perceptions at different times and in different places.

For example, in the case of religion, more interpretative approaches allow people to give voice to what religion or spirituality may mean for them, rather than having to fit their responses into pre-given categories. However an interpretative approach might still privilege the interpretation of the researcher over those of the subjects of research. Interpretative approaches acknowledge the intentionality of researchers as well as those being studied. Such approaches, especially in recent developments of these methodologies, offer more flexibility and are more likely to tolerate a multiplicity of meanings, rather than to to establish the one right answer.

SUMMARY

- Positivist methodologies are more likely to adopt approaches based on observation and quantitative methods.

- Interpretative approaches acknowledge the agency and understanding of human subjects.

- Interpretative approaches allow for different perspectives and meanings to be explored.

3 SECULARIZATION: IS RELIGION ON THE DECLINE?

The question posed by *Newsweek* discussed at the start of this chapter suggested that religious knowledge has declined in social value and status. How can we find out? What sort of evidence can we use to support or refute this claim?

Using a substantive definition of religion, it is relatively easy to gather statistics that appear to show increasing secularization in modern societies ('modern' here does not mean contemporary, but, rather, having reached an advanced state of 'modernization', particularly in the spheres of the economy, education and science). As indicated in the Introduction, levels of church attendance have been steadily declining in Europe in the post-war period.

Attendance at a place of worship is one way of attempting to measure the importance of religion. To take Christian church attendance in the UK as an example, this shows a significant decline (see Figure 2.3). The results of surveys of Christian belief are shown in Tables 2.1 and 2.2.

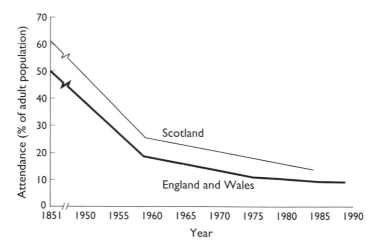

FIGURE 2.3   Adult church attendance, Britain, 1851–1989

Sources: Bruce, 1995, Figure 2.2, p.40. Data: Brierley, P., 1980, *Prospects for the Eighties: From a Census of the Churches in 1979* (London, Bible Society); Brierley, P. and Macdonald, F. 1985, *Prospects for Scotland: From a Census of the Churches in 1984* (Edinburgh, The Bible Society of Scotland); Brierley, P. 1991, *Prospects for the Nineties: Trends and Tables from the English Church Census* (London, MARC Europe); British Parliamentary Papers, *1851 Census, Great Britain, Report and Tables on Religious Worship 1852–3* (reprinted by Irish University Press, 1970); British Parliamentary Papers, *Religious Worship and Education, Scotland, Report and Tables* (London, HMSO, 1854)

TABLE 2.1 Belief may be more difficult to measure than church attendance, but people have been asked: Belief in God, Britain and Northern Ireland, 1991

	Position	Britain (%)	Northern Ireland (%)
'I don't believe in God'	1	10	1
'I don't know whether there is a God and I don't believe there is any way to find out'	2	14	4
'I don't believe in a personal God but I do believe in a higher power of some kind'	3	13	4
'I find myself believing in God some of the time but not at others'	4	13	7
'While I have doubts, I feel that I do believe in God'	5	26	20
'I know God really exists and I have no doubts about it'	6	23	57
'I don't know' and 'No answer'	7	2	7

Sources: Bruce, 1995, Table 2.10, p.49. Data: *British Social Attitudes Survey*, 1991

TABLE 2.2 The question of what religious belief means to people has also been surveyed: 'What is God?', Britain, 1947–87 (%)

	1947	1957	1987
'There is a personal God'	45	41	37
'There is some sort of spirit or vital force which controls life'	39	37	42
'I am not sure that there is any sort of God or life force'	16	–	–
'I don't know what to think'	–	16	–
'I don't really think there is any sort of spirit/ god or life force'	–	6	–
'Don't know', other, or neither	–	–	21

Sources: Bruce, 1995, Table 2.12, p.50. Data: Gallup, G.H. (ed.), 1976, *The Gallup International Public Opinion Polls; Great Britain 1937–1975* (New York, Random House); Svennevig, M., Haldane, I., Speirs, S. and Gunter, B. 1989, *Godwatching: Viewers, Religion and Television* (London, John Libbey/IBA)

ACTIVITY 2.3

How useful are such survey findings? Which kind of definition of religion underpins this collection of evidence? What else might we need to know in seeking to assess the secularization claim?

COMMENT _____

Surveys of religious belief are not quite so clear-cut as those measuring church attendance. In Britain, 75 per cent believed in a supernatural power (Table 2.1), but the opinion polls showed a fall in belief in a personal God, down from 45 per cent in 1947 to 37 per cent in 1987, although there had been an increase in belief in 'some sort of spirit or vital force which controls life' from 39 per cent to 42 per cent in the same period (Table 2.2). The latter trend may represent a drifting apart of 'orthodox Christianity' and 'popular belief', although a Mass Observation survey in 1947 – entitled significantly *Puzzled People* – also found a widespread belief in God, but not along orthodox Christian lines (Mass Observation, 1948).

There are further complicating factors. For example, figures are very different for Northern Ireland, where 57 per cent agreed with the statement 'I know God really exists and I have no doubt about it' compared with 23 per cent in Britain (Table 2.1). This suggests that religious belief may be stronger where it has relevance to the social and cultural situation, such as where there are opposing collective identities (e.g. Protestant or Catholic identities in Northern Ireland). Such an explanation has also been put forward to explain the much higher levels of religious belief and practice in the USA which, as the most modernized of societies, might be expected to be the most secularized according to the secularization thesis (88 per cent of US adults say they believe in a divine power and 31 per cent report attending religious services on a weekly or almost weekly basis (NORC, 1999)). America has experienced successive waves of immigrant groups, each of which has sought to define its identity in terms of its distinctive cultural characteristics, including religion. In other words, religion can still serve a functional role for individuals and groups in even the most modern societies, although there may be more than one 'sacred canopy' in a modern, multicultural, pluralist society.

Statistical evidence depends largely upon a substantive definition of religion, focusing as it does on the practice of worshippers and believers and the content of the religion. There are, however, aspects of people's experience and understanding of religion which are difficult if not impossible to assess by quantifiable survey techniques. There are other questions which can be asked which could extend to other beliefs and practices outside those of formal or established religion. There are also more qualitative approaches to research which seek to interpret people's experiences of religion and spirituality by probing more deeply into their understanding and the language they use to express it. Indeed, attendance at a place of worship may not in itself indicate religious belief. Individuals may participate in the rites of passage in the established Church of England – for example, weddings or christenings – for social and cultural reasons rather than those of deeply held religious belief.

According to the substantive definition of religion, there seems to have been a general process of secularization as part of the modernization process (although less so in the USA, where levels of church attendance and religious belief remain high). We can turn our attention now to examining those situations which seem to run contrary to that trend. Or, to put it another way, we can adopt a more inclusive definition of religion and examine how belief systems which include some of the characteristics associated with religion function to offer meaning and identity in certain situations and for particular groups. One way of doing this, as we have suggested, is to undertake an interpretative analysis. The examples we have chosen are: gender and religion; ethnicity and religion; and New Age beliefs and practices (e.g. the new ecology).

SUMMARY

- There is some evidence that UK society has become more secularized.
- Such evidence depends largely on a substantive definition of religion.
- The evidence is not clear-cut; there are differences across the UK and among different groups.
- We may need different sorts of evidence – qualitative, interpretative evidence as well as quantitative evidence.

4   GENDER AND RELIGION

TABLE 2.3   Gender and church attendance, Britain and Northern Ireland, 1991 (%)

Attendance	Britain		Northern Ireland	
	Men	Women	Men	Women
Frequent	37	63	39	61
Regular	35	65	57	43
Rare	48	52	49	51

Sources: Bruce, 1995, Table 2.8, p.43. Data: *British Social Attitudes Survey*, 1991

The question of religious knowledge and its meanings may be different for women because of their different experiences, both as participants in religious practices and in other spheres of life. For example, although empirical evidence suggests that women play an important part in the informal side of church organization, and that their attendance at Christian churches is higher than that of men in the contemporary UK, the bureaucratic structures of most of the UK's churches and other religious institutions are dominated by men (Knott, 1994). This raises some interesting questions. Firstly, is the greater participation by women only the case for particular religious institutions in the UK – namely, Christian churches? Secondly, what does religion mean for the women who participate at one level but are not, on the whole, involved in the hierarchies of religious organization? The two questions are related because attendance at a particular place of worship is not equally required of women and men in all religions; for example, for many women in Islam religious observance and practice take place within the home, making it more difficult to evaluate and measure women's participation in religious life. Such empirical evidence does not give us a complete picture, although it does provide a starting point for investigation; and, more importantly, it does not give any insight into the meanings which religion may have for those who are involved. Although women have not occupied public roles in the administrative hierarchies of most of the religions in the UK, they have played a significant part in religious life. For example, the arrival of women from South Asia in the 1960s had a considerable impact on the practice of Islam, Hinduism and Sikhism in the UK, shaping domestic religious activities and encouraging the establishment of places of worship such as mosques and gurdwaras (Knott,

FIGURE 2.4 The Reverend Veronica Hayden performing a baptism in east London, 1992

1994). Even though women did not participate on the management committees of these institutions, nor as representatives of their faith in the public arena, it was often women who felt the need to retain their religious identities and to maintain links with their own religious identifications.

Christian churches in the UK have also seen the impact of women's involvement; for example, in challenging male dominance of the priesthood in the Anglican church, and in arguing for the use of more 'inclusive' language in liturgy. The traditional Anglican creed, for instance, states that Christ died 'for us men', rather than 'for us' or 'us human beings', which would be more inclusive. The other significant change was the eventual decision by the Synod of the Church of England in 1992 to admit women to the priesthood. Branches of Judaism (but not orthodox Judaism) had already admitted women as rabbis and some Christian denominations had permitted women to the ministry long before – for example, Baptists, in 1922. However, much of women's participation in religion takes place outside the public arena; that is, outside either the place of worship or of public debate. How can social scientists attempt to investigate this? How might religious worship and practice be gendered? What strategies are there for interrogating the meaning which religion has for women in particular?

One of the most obvious approaches is to allow women to speak for themselves; for example, through the kind of interview which encourages women to give voice to their own experiences. Women are able to describe the roles which they have or to express the meanings which religious life has for them. Jewish women have described the importance of family and of tradition and of the woman's role in introducing children to their religion (Jewish Women in London Group, 1989).

FIGURE 2.5 Rabbi Alexandra Wright (on the right) after conducting a Sabbath service at Radlett and Bushey Reform Synagogue

Much of the interview material which records women's experiences of religion within the home focuses on women's relationships with their children and on their experience of having children. Kim Knott argues that it may be more useful to talk about *spirituality* than religion, in order to broaden the debate and to allow respondents to express concern with this dimension of experience. Some women describe childbirth as a spiritual experience: 'In giving birth to my first child I had an experience which was to be the beginning of a different understanding of the ground of our spiritual being ... I felt I was taking part in the enormous act of creation' (Quaker Women's Group, 1986, pp.38–9).

Being involved in the creation of human life is also associated with the conservation of the natural world, according to women's responses to questioning about their experiences (Kroll, 1987). This suggests that to classify these experiences as 'religious' may be too constraining, although it would be wrong to prejudge religion as only including that which occurs within the framework of formal religious organizations.

Women's expressions of spirituality are also manifest in their actions. As suggested above, women have been involved in collective activity to challenge the constraints of formal religion. In addition to collections of women's experiences in oral histories, it is also the case that fiction, including novels and poetry, can offer another resource for exploring subjective experience and provide additional voices.

A broadening of our understanding of the concept of spirituality provides a more inclusive classification of what can be called religious knowledge. For example, some woman-centred spiritual movements such as eco-feminism bridge the gap between politics and religion:

> Eco-feminism is a new term for an ancient wisdom. As women in various movements – ecology, peace, feminist and especially health – rediscovered the interdependence and connectedness of everything, they also discovered what was called spiritual dimension of life – the realization of this interconnectedness was itself sometime called spirituality. Capitalist and Marxist materialism, both of which saw the achievement of human happiness as basically conditional on the expansion of material goods' production, denied or denigrated this dimension.

> The desire to recover, to regenerate [this] wisdom as a means to liberate women and nature from patriarchal destruction also motivated this turning towards spirituality. The term 'spiritual' is ambiguous, it means different things to different people. For some it means a kind of religion, but not one based upon the continuation of the patriarchal, monotheistic religions of Christianity, Judaism or Islam, all of which are arguably hostile to women and to nature *vis-à-vis* their basic warrior traditions.

> (Mies and Shiva, 1997, p.500)

ACTIVITY 2.4

Is the eco-feminist movement a challenge to religious certainties?

What are the implications of the above quotation from Mies and Shiva for the claim, that religion is in decline, with which we started this chapter? Might women's involvement in religion support or refute the claim that the UK is becoming a more secular society?

COMMENT _____

The empirical evidence with which we started this section suggests that women may be more involved in church attendance in some religions than men. However, things may be more complicated with respect to whether this affects their understanding of religious knowledge and meanings. We have argued that we need additional evidence to find out the meanings which religion has for women. If we ask questions about women's participation in religion, this raises further questions about what we mean by religion and how religious knowledge is defined, as well as about how we as social scientists go about finding out what religion means to women in the contemporary UK. The brief discussion in this section has suggested that we need a broader definition of religious knowledge than one which is confined to formal, organized religion and that we need to extend our investigations beyond what can be observed or measured and to attempt to find out how women see religion themselves – what it means to them. Interpretative approaches offer more scope for women to express their own understanding of religion, rather than to comply with pre-given categories of questionnaires or have their beliefs measured by observable behaviour.

SUMMARY

- The specific example of women and religion offers a more complex picture of religious knowledge and religion in the UK.

- Empirical evidence suggests that women may have greater involvement than men in some religions.

- Such data does not provide us with information about how women perceive their own involvement; we need a more interpretative approach.

- Women may offer their own understanding of spiritual experience which challenges orthodox, patriarchal religion.

5 ETHNICITY AND RELIGION

Religion and ethnicity are enmeshed. Ethnicity offers another aspect of diversity in exploring religious knowledge and meaning in the UK. Whose religious knowledge are we discussing?

The UK is a multifaith, multiethnic society. The Church of England may still be the established church but it is certainly not the only form of religion. The diversity of religious forms in the UK challenges the privileging of any particular form at the end of the twentieth century (see Table 2.4).

Ethnicity is another factor that complicates the picture as far as secularization is concerned. Ethnicity has been defined as a segment of a society 'whose members are thought, by themselves and/or others, to have a common origin

FIGURE 2.6 Hindus celebrating Diwali (New Year) Ceremony of Light in north London, 1998

TABLE 2.4   Community size: total religious community in millions, Britain, 1975–95

	1975	1980	1985	1990	1992	1995[a]
Anglicans[b]	27.2[c]	27.1[c]	27.0	26.9	26.8	26.7
Baptist[e]	0.6	0.6	0.6	0.6	0.6	0.6
Roman Catholic[b]	5.5[c]	5.5[c]	5.6[c]	5.6[c]	5.6	5.6
Independent[e]	0.5	0.5	0.6	0.8	0.7	0.7
Methodist	1.6	1.5	1.3	1.3	1.3	1.3
Orthodox	0.4	0.4	0.4	0.5	0.5	0.5
Other churches[e]	0.3	0.3	0.3	0.3	0.3	0.3
Pentecostal[e]	0.2	0.3	0.3	0.3	0.3	0.4
Presbyterian	1.9	1.7	1.7	1.6	1.5	1.5
TOTAL Trinitarian churches	38.2	37.9	37.8	37.9	37.6	37.6
Church of Scientology	0.1[c]	0.2[c]	0.3[c]	0.3[c]	0.3	0.4
Other non-Trinitarian churches[e]	0.5[c]	0.5[c]	0.5[c]	0.6[c]	0.6	0.6
Hindus	0.3[c]	0.4[c]	0.4[c]	0.4	0.4	0.4
Jews	0.4	0.3[c]	0.3	0.3	0.3	0.3
Muslims	0.4[c]	0.6[c]	0.9[d]	1.0[c]	1.1	1.1
Sikhs[e]	0.2	0.3[c]	0.3[c]	0.5	0.5	0.6
Other religions	0.1	0.2	0.3	0.3	0.3	0.3
TOTAL non-Trinitarian and other religions	2.0	2.5	3.0	3.4	3.5	3.7
TOTAL all religions	40.2	40.4	40.8	41.3	41.1	41.3
Percentage of population:						
Trinitarian churches	68%[c]	67%[c]	67%[c]	66%	65%	64%
Non-Trinitarian churches and other religions	4%	5%	5%	6%	6%	7%
Total all religions	72%[c]	72%[c]	72%[c]	72%[c]	71%	71%

[a] Estimate
[b] Baptised membership
[c] Revised figure
[d] 852.900 more exactly
[e] Taken as approximately double membership
Sources: Davie, 1994, Table 4.2, p.48; adapted from Brierley and Hiscock, 1993, p.282

and to share important segments of a common culture and who, in addition, participate in shared activities in which the common origin and culture are significant ingredients' (Yinger, 1976, p.200). But how exactly an ethnic group is labelled depends on how others see it and how it sees itself at a particular time and in relation to the situation – no ethnic group has an 'essential character' that unambiguously defines it. In other words, ethnicity is 'relational'; it depends on the situation. For example, labels such as 'Pakistani', 'Asian', 'Black', 'Muslim', 'White', 'Christian' may be attached to or by the same group of people depending on the situation. Religion may be the key defining feature of a particular ethnic group, or religion may offer one feature shared by several ethnic groups. The need to include religious affiliation was recognised in the 2001 UK census. It is significant that, in recent years, some of the most controversial struggles have been over religious labels. On the one hand, it may be a struggle for religious recognition:

> The defining of immigrant groups without reference to religious identities – largely a consequence of the view of religion as a matter of private life, not collective action or public policy – certainly has generated the charge among some Muslims in Britain that secular multiculturalism seeks to deliberately emasculate Muslim communities. Muslims in Britain, for example, feel particularly aggrieved that while racial discrimination and incitement to racial hatred are unlawful, religious discrimination and incitement to religious hatred is unlawful only in Northern Ireland.
>
> (Modood and Werbner, 1997, p.8)

On the other hand, one reason why certain British citizens, whose families came from Asia, may feel it is necessary to adopt a religious label as an identity is that it is this characteristic that is being used to identify them as different from the majority, and so as 'other'. Ever since the attacks on the World Trade Centre and the Pentagon in 2001, in what came to be known as 9/11, and subsequent fears of global terrorism, for example associated with Al Qu'eda, an image of Islam as a violent, fundamentalist faith that sets itself apart from Western liberal society has existed in many Western countries. Consequently, one interpretation of the tendency to accept the label of Muslim might be as a form of defensive solidarity in the face of religious discrimination and racism. However, another interpretation is that Muslims are taught that the brotherhood/sisterhood of Islam embraces all ethnicities equally (although you may have noticed in the above quotation that loss of power is described specifically in gendered terms –'emasculate', rather than using the more neutral term 'disempower'). Sometimes this is developed into a conscious anti-ethnicity approach in which it is insisted that the 'imagined community' of Moslems (*umnah*) takes precedence over what are regarded as merely ethnic and national heritages. More positively, 'fundamentalism' can be understood as 'new religious politics' (Keddie, 1999), providing the focus for resistance to, for example, colonial, ethnocentric cultures and racism. (Classifying religious beliefs as 'fundamentalist' is, however, highly contentious, since it may itself involve racist assumptions.)

Ethnicity
'Ethnicity' refers to a group or community seen as sharing culture and history. 'Ethnicity' refers to everybody, although sometimes it is used as if white people did not belong to an ethnic group.

Some surveys carried out in Britain found that Muslims responded to a question about identity by putting religion down as their core social identity before mentioning that they were of Pakistani or Bangladeshi origin (Modood *et al.*, 1994, p.62). By contrast, respondents of Afro-Caribbean descent did not feel marked apart on the basis of religion – after all, their Christian religion is that of the majority (Modood *et al.*, 1994, p.57). In this case, the interpretation of the function served by the belief system was less to do with a sense of 'difference' and 'otherness'. The Afro-Caribbean people expressed a more individualistic view of religion, speaking of the contribution of religion to coping with worries and the pressures of life, and emphasizing the therapeutic and celebratory nature of religious practices.

It is clear that religion can articulate with ethnicity in various ways and serve a variety of functions. It can help minority groups, as well as the majority ethnic groups that have numerical as well as status dominance, to define their identity symbolically, as well as giving meaning to their experiences of marginality – either as a group or individually. The revival or reassertion of religion in such circumstances may be one of the responses at the local level to globalization, which may seem to threaten minority cultures with extinction, and so provoke a conscious defensive (and defiant) reaction. The result in terms of ethnic identity is that a **diaspora** will use religion as part of its hybrid or hyphenated identity (e.g. British-Muslim). This entails 're-remembering' and 're-creating' the disparate elements that make up such a hybrid cultural identity. Not only does this involve dealing with practical problems, such as adapting the religion to a new life, including sexuality and relations with the opposite sex, but it also includes negotiating the meaning of the religion with fellow religionists of different origins. It is for this reason that the public impression of a minority religion may be that it is controversial and the mass media will give prominence to 'extreme' (often untypical) elements, such as 'fundamentalism' and the insistence on distinctive practices – as in the case of some Muslim women wearing the veil.

Diaspora
People living outside their alleged common land of group origin, such as African or Jewish people around the world, or a Muslim or Hindu group in Britain.

One conclusion of studies of different ethnic groups and religions in Britain is that second-generation members are less religious than their parents' generation, which would tend to support the secularization thesis. However, the ethnic groups vary in the importance that they attach to religion as part of their cultural identity. For example, second-generation Muslims are more likely to attach importance to their religious identity than Afro-Caribbeans (Modood *et al.*, 1994). Furthermore, although the contrast between generations gives some support to the secularization thesis, religion still plays a significant part in the culture of most ethnic groups. This suggests that religion can still serve a group function, especially for groups who experience marginalization, in even the most secularized of modern societies.

On the whole, however, religion has become more a matter of individual choice in modern societies – a cultural resource that individuals can draw on to give meaning to their experiences or to fill a need.

SUMMARY

- Religious belief has different significance for the different ethnic groups which make up the UK.
- Assertion of religious identity may be more important than ethnic or other identities for some groups; for example, Islam embraces several national, or ethnic identities.
- Religious identity may be especially important to combat racist stereotypes.
- Religion can be involved in the processes of racialization and ethnicization.

6 NEW AGE BELIEFS

One of the areas in which there seems to have been a rapid growth of belief in spiritual powers is that of New Age beliefs and practices. The extent of these beliefs is difficult to calculate in statistical terms because they are not based in churches or sects with registered members. It is often a case of individuals reading certain kinds of literature or engaging in practices in private. Some estimates have been made based on books published between 1970 and 1990. The total number of titles on the occult grew by 150 per cent (Bruce, 1995, p.104). A further problem is that there is no strict definition of New Age.

What do you think of as New Age beliefs? What would you include under this heading?

New Age can range from alternative medicine and green issues to meditation and therapy. One publisher's list of subjects included all of the following: 'Alchemy, Astrology, ... Myth, Dreamwork, Earth Mysteries, Feng Sui, Herbalism, Human Potential, Meditation, Mysticism, Natural Magic, Pendulum Dowsing, Prophecy, Psychosynthesis, Shamanism, Sufism, Taoism, Aborigine Tradition, Chakras, The Goddess, The Grail Tradition, Greek Tradition, Qabalah, Visualization, Zen' (Bruce, 1995, p.105).

A formulation of the basic assumptions of New Age thinking is provided by Jeremy Tarcher. It dwells on the 'place of humanity in the cosmos' and is summarized as follows:

1 The world, including the human race, constitutes an expression of a higher, more comprehensive divine nature.

2 Hidden within each human being is a higher divine self, which is a manifestation of the higher, more comprehensive divine nature.

3   This higher nature can be awakened and can become the centre of the
individual's everyday life.

4   This awakening is the reason for the existence of each individual life.

(quoted in Heelas, 1996, p.226)

FIGURE 2.7   'Tinkers' Bubble' collective, Somerset, 1999: the challenge of the new
'alternative' lifestyles

Sociologists of religion take different views about the significance of New Age
phenomena. One view is that they provide further evidence that the sacred
does not disappear in modern society, but simply takes new forms, and also
that the very weakness of institutionalized religion has made it easier for the
sacred to be plundered by the secular and put to new uses (Davie, 1994,
p.41). An example of plundering is that of the human potential movement,
which has adapted religious ideas about spiritual development and used them
for management training (Heelas, 1996). Two examples of alternative lifestyles
with a religious dimension, where the religious seems to have spilled over into
the secular world, are complementary medicine and the more radical versions
of the ecological movement. Alternative medicine frequently concerns itself
with the whole person – mind, body and spirit. As Grace Davie puts it: '"Holy"
and "whole" have reacquired their common root; the set-apart or the sacred
becomes once more integral to the well-being of the individual in question, for
no healing can take place while mind, body and soul remain fragmented'
(Davie, 1994, p.40). In Davie's view, holistic approaches incorporate spirituality
rather than attempting to draw distinctions between religious, scientific and
moral knowledges, as if each was a pure, discrete category.

Similarly, in the view of some ecologists, the well-being of the planet
depends on a right relationship between its parts, and humanity is required to

restore its true relationship as part of the creative process, rather than setting itself up as master of the process and at liberty to exploit the earth's resources at will. Once the true relationship is restored, it is argued than the health of the whole will be enhanced. As an American commentator observed:

> The new ethically oriented environmental movement seethes with such unprecedented ideas. The self-styled 'deep ecologists' are advancing 'ecological egalitarianism'. An educator discusses abuse of the environment in terms of 'prejudice against nature' and relates it explicitly to racial, sexual, national and economic prejudice. He aspires to nothing less than liberating the earth. Ecotheologians recommend a morality based on the 'spiritual democracy' of God's creation, including everything from subatomic particles to spiral nebulae. One Christian environmentalist is prepared to defend the 'inalienable rights' of all the 'citizens' in a Kingdom of God expanded to the entire ecosystem. A Pulitzer prize-winning poet calls for an 'ultimate democracy' in which plants and animals join people as rights holders. The journal *Environmental Law* carries an essay proposing a constitutional amendment stating that wildlife must not be deprived of 'life, liberty or habitat without due process of law'. Clearly the old boundaries that limited liberalism to human freedom are breaking down.
>
> (Nash, 1989, p.6)

By contrast to the argument that sees New Age beliefs in terms of the sacred spreading over into secular spheres, there is the view that New Age thought is shaped by a mishmash of scientific and pseudo-scientific ideas. According to Steve Bruce, many New Agers combine criticism of the scientific and medical establishments with the belief that they are doing what will someday be recognized as science. They maintain that scientific explanations are not yet available because prejudice and professional interest prevent scientists from asking the right questions. However, the difference between conventional science and the New Age is explained by Bruce by reference to the anthropologist E. Evans-Pritchard's discussion of the pre-modern thought of the Zande people. Evans-Pritchard was an influential early twentieth-century anthropologist who studied non-industrialized societies.

Read the following extract by Evans-Pritchard. Could there be a scientific explanation of this event?

> In Zandeland sometimes an old granary collapses. There is nothing remarkable in this. Every Zande knows that termites eat the supports in course of time and that even the hardest woods decay after years of service. Now a granary is the summerhouse of a Zande household. People sit beneath the granary when it collapses and they are injured, for it is a heavy structure .... Now why should these particular people have been sitting under this particular granary at the particular moment when it collapsed? .... We say that the granary collapsed because its supports were eaten away by termites. That is the cause that explains the collapse of the granary. We also say that people were sitting under it at the time because it was the heat of the day and they thought it would be a comfortable place to talk

and work. This is the cause of people being under the granary at the time it collapsed. To our minds the only relationship between these two independently caused facts is their coincidence in time and space. We have no explanations of why the two chains of causation intersected at a certain time and in a certain place, for there is no interdependence between them.

(Evans-Pritchard, 1937; quoted in Bruce, 1995, pp.209–10)

The Zande are not prepared to leave things without explanation. They have other reasons that give moral meaning to such events – witchcraft. The question is, why were these particular people injured? The Zande suggest a malevolent force caused them to be selected, incited by witchcraft. Their explanation emphasizes the importance of moral meanings.

Science offers no techniques for discovering moral meanings and so there will always be a gap for knowledge such as that offered by New Age. The secularization thesis sometimes seemed to suggest that the gap left for religious knowledge would continue to diminish as science progressed. However, although people may become accustomed to looking to science for explanations in modern society and this may have the knock-on effect of diminishing the authority of religious knowledge, strictly speaking nothing has changed as science could never claim to offer moral meanings.

In some ways, New Age spirituality might be seen as a response to modernization, secularization and globalization, all of which have been fostered by science. As a reaction against authority based on communal agreement, whether the community of scientists or that of organized religion, New Agers tend to locate authority within the individual self. They usually prioritize personal experience over institutionalized beliefs and they may even claim for personal spirituality a potential for the kind of 'progress' and 'evolution' usually associated with science. New Age beliefs may be one way in which contemporary religion attempts to create a dialogue with science and, correspondingly, some scientists have been attracted by its holistic and spiritually integrative emphasis. Such beliefs also transcend some of the boundaries between sets of knowledge, bridging the distinction between science and religion.

SUMMARY

- There was an increase in New Age beliefs in the latter part of the twentieth century in the UK.

- This could be an example of new forms of religion and thus it challenges secularization.

- New Age beliefs can, however, take the form of challenging scientific orthodoxies rather than just those of the established religions and seek to become new science rather than the new religion.

- New Age beliefs illustrate the interconnections between different sets of knowledge.

6.1 Science and the extrasensory

Some social scientists maintain that what has really happened to religion in modern society is that people continue to believe without belonging to religious organizations. (Grace Davie's leading textbook in the sociology of religion is titled *Religion in Britain Since 1945: Believing without Belonging*, 1994). Others argue that the authority of science and the materialistic nature of secular thought leads people to suppress any tendency to give religious meaning or attach religious discourses to their experiences of the extraordinary. It was this latter belief that led a retired professor of zoology at Oxford University, Alister Hardy, to set up a Religious Experience Research Unit at Manchester College, Oxford, in 1969, which advertised in the newspapers for people to send in accounts of experiences of being in touch with a reality beyond the self. The question the Unit asked was: 'Have you ever been aware of or influenced by a presence or power, whether you call it God or not, which is different from your everyday self?' They soon had 3,000 positive replies, which Hardy proceeded to classify into subdivisions, in a procedure similar to that he had used as a zoologist. In this case, the subdivisions were related to the five senses (omitting the 'taste' category, which had no responses, but adding a 'sixth sense' – supposed extrasensory perception, including telepathy, precognition, clairvoyance, contact with the dead and apparitions). The first category was 'visual experience of a sensory or quasi-sensory nature'. This included cases where people believed they had had a vision, or perhaps seen a bright light, or felt themselves surrounded by light. A second category was 'auditory'. In this case people felt that they had heard a voice, perhaps calming or guiding them. A third category was 'touch', and a fourth – in practice a very small group – was where people felt that they had smelt something in a supernatural way. Among the 'triggers' of these experiences, the most common were natural beauty, participation in religious worship, prayer or meditation, music, literature and dreams, depression or despair. The most frequently recorded effects were a sense of security, of protection or peace, a sense of joy or happiness, a sense of guidance, vocation or inspiration, a sense of certainty, clarity or enlightenment, a sense of integration, wholeness or fulfilment (Hay, 1990, p.41).

A fellow scientist, David Hay, subsequently set up a Religious Experience Research Project at Nottingham University, which used questionnaires and interviews to follow-up the work begun by Hardy at Oxford. He found, in 1976, that over a third of all adults in Britain claim to have had experience of this kind. Generally speaking women were rather more likely to claim these experiences than men, in the ratio of four to three, and as one moves up the social scale, more people were willing to talk about religious experience. Also, the more education people had, the more likely they were to talk about their experiences. As with church attendance, the 'higher' social classes were found to score more positively on the scale than the 'lower' classes. In other words, contrary to what has sometimes been claimed, supernatural belief does not seem to be stronger among working-class people and the less educated. When questioned about their happiness, it seemed that the happier people were, the more likely they were to claim such experiences. A larger follow-up survey through Gallup Poll, in 1986, found that almost half those questioned had had such an experience, and if one included responses claiming some sort of premonition as a religious experience, then the total rose to two-thirds of the respondents. An interesting methodological point is that, if the investigators carried out hour-long, in-depth interviews, rather than brief interviews with an opinion pollster, the percentage admitting to some kind of religious experience rose to over 60 per cent in one survey and 40 per cent in another.

Hay argues that people are embarrassed to disclose such experiences in today's supposedly secular society and that the whole complex of imagery at the heart of popular culture implies a repression of religion among ordinary people. He blames the pervasive presence of a crude version of nineteenth-century positivist science, which leads people to believe that the only authoritative knowledge is that derived by scientists from experimental research, even though many sophisticated scientists would be more tentative about their claims. Interestingly, to back up his point, Hay quotes the findings of an experiment carried out by the American psychologist, Stanley Milgram, in 1963, which showed that ordinary people will obediently perform what appear to be horrifying experiments (like administering a severe electric shock) on their fellow human beings, simply because a 'scientist' in a white lab coat requests it: 'They feel unable to refuse such an authority figure. It must be obvious that the much larger step of refusing to accept the interpretations of reality held by a dominant scientific culture requires either remarkable self-confidence or the presence of a protective ghetto' (Hay, 1990, p.60).

This is a controversial position and one that many social scientists would want to question. At one extreme it could suggest that all knowledge is of equal validity and that we should give no more credence to the statements of scientists than to any other group or individual. This would deny the possibility that social scientists, including those studying religious experiences, can advance knowledge by subjecting people's accounts of their experiences to rigorous analysis and comparison with similar phenomena. On the other hand, it could have the salutary effect of making us less inclined to overlook or dismiss people's accounts of experiences which do not fit conventional assumptions – they are the assumptions of secular culture or those of social scientists who regard secularization as an inevitable process. It might also be worth stating that, as the general population becomes more educated, they are able to be more critical and informed about the limitations of science, and also aware that scientists often disagree. The recent controversies about genetically-modified food are a good example.

SUMMARY

- Surveys have shown that large numbers of adults in the UK claim to have had extrasensory experiences.
- In-depth interviews led to more disclosures of such experiences.
- There may be a reluctance to admit to extrasensory or spiritual experiences in a society where scientific rationalism is seen as dominant.
- Such evidence may challenge the secularization thesis.

7 CONCLUSION

This chapter has used religious knowledge as an example of an area of enquiry within the social sciences. Religion is thus used to illustrate some of the methods used by social scientists. Religious knowledge has a particular status; it has been defined as referring to that which is held sacred and set apart from the everyday routine of our lives. Religious knowledge has been constructed as different from scientific knowledge. Religious knowledge is produced within different areas of human experience and in different ways from scientific knowledge. Religion has been seen as revelatory knowledge whereas science has been presented as empirically susceptible to proof or falsification and subject to the rationality of natural science. This makes religion a challenging area for social sciences investigation. The secularization thesis has been presented as the decline of religion in the face of the contemporary dominance of science. We have argued that the position is more complex. Firstly, religious knowledge is located at many different sites; it covers a wide range of experiences and understandings which might more usefully be categorized as spirituality. Spirituality can encompass a range of different sets of knowledge, including combinations of religion and science. Secondly, an interpretative approach which explores the functions served by religion and people's perception of religious knowledge suggests that, whilst some religious practice may be in decline in the UK, this trend towards secularization can be challenged in a number of ways and the real situation may me more varied and complex. Changes in the status of religious knowledge offer uncertainties and diverse new opportunities. Women are challenging the patriarchal hierarchies of organized religion and offering their own conceptions of spirituality. A multifaith society embraces a diversity of religions which have different meanings for their respective followers. Gender and ethnicity combine together in shaping the experience and take-up of religion and spirituality. New Age knowledge offers an extension of religious experience as well as challenging established religions. People are renegotiating religious and spiritual knowledge and resisting the constraints of traditional religious structures. The production of religious knowledge offers opportunities for agency, both individual and collective. Religious knowledge still has a place in the contemporary UK. It may supplement scientific knowledge and address the spiritual and ethical questions not answered by science. There is also overlap between the knowledge which is categorized as religion and that which is scientific, especially if a functionalist definition of religion is adopted. There is evidence to support the secularization thesis, but the claims of this thesis have to be critically evaluated. These claims raise further questions about definitions of religion. A more inclusive definition of religion, extended to encompass spirituality, raises questions about the extent of secularization and illustrates the interrelationship between different sets of knowledge.

This exploration of religious knowledge has enabled us to examine some of the different ways in which social scientists investigate the social construction of knowledge. Positivist approaches based on methods associated with the natural sciences have been adopted in, for example, providing quantitative evidence of attendance at places of religious worship. These have necessarily been complemented by more interpretative approaches which accommodate the specific features of religious and spiritual knowledge. Quantitative methods cannot access the subjectivities of belief, and social scientists have had to find ways of enabling the subjects of their investigation to speak for themselves.

REFERENCES

Armstrong, K. (1999) 'Where has God gone?', *Newsweek*, 12 July, pp.56–7.

Berger, P. (1967) *The Sacred Canopy*, New York, Doubleday.

Berger. P. (1969) *The Social Reality of Religion*, London, Faber & Faber.

Bellah, R. (1970) *Beyond Belief*, New York, Harper and Row.

Brierley, P. and Hiscock, V. (eds) (1993) *UK Christian Handbook, 1994–5 edition*, London, Christian Research Association.

Bruce, S. (1995) *Religion in the Modern Britain,* Oxford, Oxford University Press.

Comte, A. (1842–53) *The Positive Philosophy of Auguste Comte* (trans. H. Martineau), London, G. Bell.

Davie, G. (1999) 'Religion' in Taylor, S. (ed.) *Sociology: Issues and Debates*, London, Macmillan.

Davie, G. (1994) *Religion in Britain Since 1945: Believing Without Belonging*, Oxford, Blackwell.

Davie, G. (2000) *Religion in Modern Europe*, Oxford, Oxford University Press.

Durkheim, E. (1912/1965) *The Elementary Forms of the Religious Life* (trans. J.W. Swain), New York, Free Press.

Evans-Pritchard, E.E. (1937) *Witchcraft, Oracles and Magic among the Azande*, Oxford, Clarendon Press.

Hay, D. (1990) *Religious Experience Today*, London, Mobray.

Heelas, P. (1996) *The New Age Movement*, Oxford, Blackwell.

Jewish Women in London Group (1989) *Generations of Memories: Voices of Jewish Women*, The Women's Press, London.

Keddie, N. (1999) 'The new religious politics and women worldwide. A comparative study', *Journal of Women's History*, winter, February.

Knott, K. (1994) 'Women and religion in post-war Britain' in Parsons, G. (ed.) *The Growth of Religious Diversity: Britain from 1945*, Volume 2, *Issues*, London, Routledge.

Kroll, U. (1987) 'A womb-centred life' in Hurcombe, L. (ed.) *Sex and God: Some Varieties of Women's Religious Experience*, London, Routledge and Kegan Paul.

Marx, K. (1844/undated) *Contribution to the Critique of Hegel's Philosophy of Right* in Marx, K. and Engels, F. *On Religion*, Moscow, Foreign Languages Publishing House.

Mass Observation (1948) *Puzzled People: A Study of Popular Attitudes to Religion, Ethics, Progress and Politics in a London Borough*, London, Victor Gollancz.

Mies, M. and Shiva, V. (1997) 'Ecofeminism' in Kemp, S. and Squires, J. (eds) *Feminisms*, Oxford, Oxford University Press.

Modood, T., Beishon, S. and Virdee, S. (1994) *Changing Ethnic Identities*, London, Policy Studies Institute.

Modood, T. and Werbner, P. (1997) *The Politics of Multiculturalism in the New Europe*, London, Zed Books.

Nash, R.F. (1989) *The Rights of Nature*, Madison, WI, University of Wisconsin Press.

NORC (1999) *General Social Surveys, 1972–1998: Cumulative Codebook*, Chicago, IL, National Opinion Research Center.

Quaker Women's Group (1986) *Bringing the Invisible into the Light*, Quaker Home Service, London.

Thompson, K. (1976) *Auguste Comte: The Foundation of Sociology*, London, Thomas Nelson.

Weber, M. (1904/1930) *The Protestant Ethnic and the Spirit of Capitalism* (trans. T. Parsons), London, Allen and Unwin.

Woodward, K. (2004) 'Questions of identity' in Woodward, K. (ed.).

Woodward, K. (ed.) (2004) *Questioning Identity: Gender, Class, Ethnicity* (2nd edn), London, Routledge/The Open University.

Yinger, J.M. (1976) 'Ethnicity in complex societies: structural, cultural and characterological factors' in Coser, L.A. and Larsen, O.N. (eds) *The Uses of Controversy in Sociology*, New York, Free Press.

FURTHER READING

To explore further some of the debates introduced in this chapter, we suggest Grace Davie's (2000) *Religion in Modern Europe*, Oxford, Oxford University Press, which provides a contemporary critique of the role of religion and status of religious knowledge in Europe, whereas her *Religion in Britain Since 1945: Believing Without Belonging* (Oxford, Blackwell) focuses on changes in the post-war UK. Steve Bruce's (1995) *Religion in the Modern Britain*, Oxford, Oxford University Press, presents a challenge to Davie's view. Kim Knott's (1994) 'Women and religion in post-war Britain', in Parsons, G. (ed.) *The Growth of Religious Diversity: Britain from 1945*, London, Routledge, also concentrates on the UK, but particularly on the gendered nature of religion, providing an extensive range of evidence. Eileen Barker's (1991) *New Religious Movements*, London, HMSO, provides a survey of the impact of new religious groups in the UK, and Paul Heelas's (1996) *The New Age Movement*, Oxford, Blackwell, offers comprehensive coverage of New Age ideas and social movements.

We have only briefly gone into some of the classic texts in the sociology of religion here. To explore these a bit more fully, we suggest you try: Emile Durkheim (1912/1965) *The Elementary Forms of the Religious Life*, London, Allen and Unwin; Max Weber (1904/1930) *The Protestant Ethic and the Spirit of Capitalism*, New York, Free Press; E. Evans-Pritchard's (1930/1956) seminal anthropological account of religion, *Nuer Religion*, Oxford, Oxford University Press; Sigmund Freud's (1913/1983) psychoanalytic account of the importance of religion, *Totem and Taboo*, London, Ark Paperbacks; and Sir James George Frazer's (1890/1995) *The Golden Bough: A Study in Magic and Religion*, London, Macmillan, which offers a selection of pieces from Frazer's provocative earlier work on the role of religion, superstition and magic in the modern world.

Political ideologies and the environment

Simon Bromley

Contents

1 INTRODUCTION

This chapter explores the environmental challenge to another form of knowledge, modern political ideologies at two different but related levels. Firstly, we investigate the ability of the political ideologies to offer solutions to the practical problems of environmental degradation; secondly, we examine the ways in which environmental social and political thought – in shorthand 'green thinking' – questions modern political ideologies and seeks to provide alternative ways of thinking about the environment. This will enable us to address the question of whether the environmental challenge in the double sense used here – namely, the practical problems arising from the realities of environmental degradation and the alternative forms of knowledge and knowing suggested by green thinking – constitutes a crisis for modern political ideologies, and if it does, what are the alternatives offered by green thinking?

Let us begin by asking what we mean by 'political ideologies' and why do they matter? Political ideologies can be understood as maps of the social world which aim to tell us something about how that world works, how it might be different and how, if we wish to change it, we can get from here to there. In other words, political ideologies have a descriptive component (they tell us this is how things are), an explanatory component (they show us how things work or hang together), and a normative or prescriptive dimension (they seek to persuade us that this is how things could and should be). They are networks or frameworks of concepts linked together by history, culture and logic, formed – like other theories in the social sciences – by abstracting from the ebb and flow of social life itself, but they are grounded in our social relations and practices. Modern political ideologies, therefore, need to be aware of their own cultural, historical and theoretical preconditions. They need to be to some extent self-reflective, as well as being able to give us good reasons to follow their prescriptions, to offer us linked sets of ideas and concepts 'that enable us to choose to become what we want to become' (Freeden, 1996, p.553). This suggests that political ideologies survive and thrive or wither and die in so far as they offer accurate, useable and compelling maps *and* to the extent that the maps allow us to get to where we want to go. In short, modern political ideologies must address themselves to the level of ideas and values as well as to the realm of interests and practical achievements. As such, political ideologies should be distinguished from mere propaganda on the one side, since propaganda only has to be effective, and the more abstract and refined reflections of political philosophy or social theory on the other, since the relevant criteria for judging this kind of knowledge is whether propositions are true or false or whether they generate testable hypotheses.

Why are modern political ideologies important? We suggest in this chapter that there are three main reasons. Generally, we draw upon ideologies to make sense of our experience of the social world, as well as to formulate courses of action in relation to changing it. Political ideologies, then, are important, firstly, because they help to shape our perceptions of social reality and hence to frame patterns of collective social action, thereby potentially altering the pattern of society. Political ideologies are not only shaped by the societies in which they develop but they also react back upon those societies, directing the course of their future development. Moreover, as our map metaphor suggests, different ideologies in some senses see the world differently and suggest alternative paths that we might pursue. Ideologies thus compete with one another for our attention and allegiance, and the relations between the various political ideologies are often ones of contention and conflict. Political ideologies, therefore, are important, secondly, because we often have to choose between them, and the choices we make will have significant consequences for the kinds of society we live in. Thirdly, and perhaps most importantly of all, modern political ideologies are often able to appeal to us at a very deep level and to draw out correspondingly strong levels of individual and collective commitment. Put bluntly, people will fight for their ideological beliefs, as the often bitter ideological history of the last two hundred years has shown. In the twentieth century, two World Wars were fought over rival ideological projects for the future of European and world order, and after the Second World War a deep ideological conflict existed between East and West until the collapse of Communist ideology in the late 1980s. Political ideologies matter because they can be issues of life and death.

If ideologies are indeed as important as this, and if the main political ideologies of Western modernity – liberalism, socialism, conservatism, social democracy and feminism – are unable to cope with the environmental challenge, then we may need new maps to chart our way in the future. At the very least, the problems posed by the issues of environmental degradation suggest that the existing maps will need to be redrawn to a greater or lesser extent.

In order to pursue the nature of the environmental challenge to political ideologies in more detail, the rest of this chapter will be organized as follows. In Section 2 we look at the practical challenges to the modern political ideologies posed by the realities of environmental degradation. Then in Section 3 we consider how these political ideologies have responded to these problems. In Section 4 we consider in more detail the nature of green thinking and try to identify the ways in which it is different from, and poses an alternative to, contemporary political ideologies of modernity. Finally, in Section 5, we attempt to evaluate the positions of the modern political ideologies and of green thinking by comparing their views on how to respond to the environmental challenge.

S U M M A R Y

- Ideologies must work at the level of ideas and values; they must have a degree of coherence, they need to deliver in practice and they must be effective in some way.

- Ideologies are important because they shape our perceptions and actions, they compete with one another for our allegiance and they are able to mobilize us at a fundamental level.

- If the political ideologies of the modern world don't have solutions to environmental problems or are found wanting in the light of the critique of green thinking, then we may need to modify or renew them.

2 ENVIRONMENTAL PROBLEMS FOR POLITICAL IDEOLOGIES

There are, of course, many ways in which novel concerns about the environment call into question established modes of political thinking and practice. To simplify our investigation of this complex area, we are going to focus on three different kinds of problems generated by the realities of environmental degradation.

To begin with, we will consider modern political ideologies' dependence upon a notion of progress centred around economic growth, increasing consumption and sustained industrialization on the basis of scientific rationality. Can this kind of economic and technological development be made environmentally sustainable? Secondly, we will examine the implications of the fact that environmental questions often arise at a *global* level while the political systems charged with responding to them are *nationally* based. That is to say, we will investigate the apparent disjuncture between the national organization of politics and policy and the global nature and scope of many environmental problems (**Cochrane and Pain, 2004; McGrew, 2004**). Finally, we will ask what happens to our most basic notions of individual and collective freedom, understood in terms of *human* interests, values and rights, when the interrelations between humans and their natural environment (including both the physical environment and other species) are introduced into the picture. To what extent do environmental problems force us to confront some of our most deeply held cultural beliefs about our place on the planet and in the cosmos?

2.1   Environmentally sustainable economic growth?

A major problem posed by environmental issues is that all modern political ideologies are committed to a notion of 'progress' based on the continuous application of scientific reason to understanding the natural world and to using the knowledge generated to build technologies that control or 'master' our natural environment. On the basis of this scientific and technological progress, an idea of economic well-being has emerged that measures success in terms of the level and rate of growth of production and consumption. Producing and consuming more and more, so that those at the bottom can catch up with those at the top, is the overriding aim. Within any given society, the ideal is that, in time, all should have whatever technology can deliver; globally, the ambition is for the poorer countries in the South to attain the lifestyles currently available only in the North.

Modern political ideologies offer a variety of views as to how to maximize technological progress and economic growth, based on variable mixes of markets (favoured by liberals) and planning (advocated by socialists), but all agree that maximizing growth is important, if only because this enables us to afford other (non-economic) goods such as a healthy environment. As an editorial in *The Economist* put it: 'As people get richer, they want a cleaner environment – and they acquire the means to pay for it' (*The Economist*, 9 November 1999).

However, there are two practical problems with this approach. In the first place, our current knowledge of the causes and effects of many environmental problems is very uncertain. This may arise from the sheer complexity of the phenomenon or from the fact that we just don't yet know enough. In either case, given the potentially irreversible nature of many processes of environmental change, we may not be in a position to make judgements based solely on the available, current state of scientific knowledge. It has also been suggested that modern science is in principle incapable of understanding and explaining the totality of the natural world, that science is just one belief system that humans have used to make their way in the world, one that is, in fact, rather recent when considered historically and culturally specific when considered across the known range of human societies. Indeed, some would argue that many environmental problems are the result of our relations with the natural world being dominated by the scientific outlook and its application in technology (see Section 4.3).

One characteristic feature of environmental problems is their complexity. The chains of cause and effect ramify so widely that even when the specific details of each step in the chain are known, the total effect may be too complex to compute. Think of something as simple as today's weather. The basic physics of short-term weather change is quite simple, but this does not mean that forecasters are able to produce accurate predictions of tomorrow's weather. Imagine, then, the complexity involved in trying to estimate the effect of carbon dioxide emissions on the world's climate over the next 50 years, let alone the knock-on consequences of the ensuing climate change on human societies! In addition, it is generally accepted that some important processes of environmental change are irreversible. For example, once a species becomes extinct its unique genetic code is lost. Once we have consumed all the world's fossil fuels, we can't use them again. Moreover, some processes of change are probably subject to quite dramatic 'threshold effects'. For example, one can safely reduce the stocks of fish in a given location bit by bit with no adverse effects on the survival of the population as a whole, until a critical point is reached. Below this point, however, any further reduction in stocks may drive the species rapidly to extinction. Many scientists fear that climate change is just such a non-linear process.

This combination of complexity and potential irreversibility means that we are often operating in conditions of real uncertainty, even when the basic scientific mechanisms involved are well understood. In those many cases where the underlying science is not well understood (for example, the total effects of carbon dioxide emissions) our predicament is even more uncertain. The increasing recognition of the importance of uncertainty in environmental matters has led to the development of the **precautionary principle** as a guide to environmental policy: namely, the idea that the burden of proof for changes with environmental consequences should lie in showing that they will *not* be harmful.

The second problem is how to render economic growth environmentally benign (**Himmelweit and Simonetti, 2004**). The practical problem here is one of getting the market to incorporate the environmental consequences of economic activity into its decision making. We will examine some of the details of this in Section 3.1, but for now we merely note three main questions.

1 Can the environmental implications of economic activity be known and measured? How can we incorporate environmental consequences into our decision making if outcomes are uncertain and unknown?

2 Even supposing that we know the environmental outcomes and can measure them, how do we value them? How much is a whale worth? What price would *you* be prepared to pay to stop the rainforests being turned into furniture and cleared for cattle breeding?

3 What about the future? Future generations cannot trade in the market or participate in a planning process, so how are their interests to be incorporated into current decision making?

Precautionary principle
Instead of assuming that socially beneficial change should go ahead unless it has unacceptable environmental consequences, the precautionary principle says that proposed changes need to be shown *not* to have unacceptable environmental consequences. It is roughly equivalent to changing the burden of proof in a trial from 'innocent until proven guilty' to 'guilty until proven innocent'.

2.2 Global environmental problems and national politics

The second problem posed by environmental issues for modern political ideologies is easy to state, even if its resolution remains deeply contested. Traditional political ideologies typically take it for granted that politics operates on the terrain of a territorially-bounded nation-state. That is to say, politics is about the articulation and representation of interests, values and rights within a particular territorially-bounded community. On this basis, politics involves the formation of policies for the self-government of a particular community. This view of politics presupposes the organization of people into separate, discrete communities; in the modern world the predominant vehicle for this has been the sovereign nation-state.

Yet often environmental issues and problems are global in scope in several different ways. Many environmental problems cross national borders and become transboundary problems, even when the cause of the problem can be precisely located in a specific national territory. For example, the Chernobyl nuclear accident in 1986 occurred in the Ukraine (then part of the former Soviet Union) but the effects of the resulting radioactive pollution were felt across Europe, including by the sheep on Welsh hill farms.

FIGURE 3.1   Radioactive field near the Chernobyl atomic reactor ruins, 1986

Other environmental issues are so widespread in their causes and effects that they constitute inherently global phenomena. Thus human economic activities in every country in the world have an impact on global warming and the effects of such warming on the world's climate will also be felt everywhere. Of course, contributions to global warming as well as the likely consequences of climate change are very unevenly distributed across the globe, but no society can insulate itself from the phenomenon. Finally, some environmental questions relate to resources shared by the international community as a whole, resources that do not fall under the control or property of any single state or group of states, these include the atmosphere, the oceans and the deep-sea bed. Other resources, while located in particular places, are often argued to be part of the 'common heritage of mankind'; for example, the world's rainforests and genetic resources. Together, these resources are often called the **global commons**.

Global commons

Global commons refers to resources that are not owned or controlled by any individual country or group of countries.

It is sometimes argued that some resources which are owned and controlled by a particular group of countries (e.g. the rainforests) should be the property of all.

So there seems to be a gap between the *national* organization of politics and the resulting public policy, on the one hand, and the *global* nature and scope of many environmental problems, on the other. This tension between what has been called *environmental globalization* and the territorially-bounded politics of nation-states raises the question of whether national-level politics can cope or deal with globally situated problems. If national political systems cannot cope, if the performance of states in terms of providing environmental protection is undermined, then what will happen to the legitimacy and authority of those states and their governments?

FIGURE 3.2   Anti-World Trade Organization demonstrators parade in Seattle

2.3 Human values and the natural environment

The third practical problem posed by environmental issues for modern political ideologies concerns our place in the wider natural world. Broadly speaking, modern political ideologies treat the rest of (non-human) nature in an instrumental fashion, that is rationally, as a means to an end. Human beings and their communities are the bearers or repositories of interests, values and rights, but the rest of nature is valued and accorded an interest only in relation to human concerns. Moreover, not only do modern political ideologies treat non-human nature in a largely instrumental fashion, they also operate as if humans were not themselves part of nature, overlooking the fact that human beings have certain natural capacities. They fail to recognize that there are natural *limits*, both of 'inner' and 'outer' nature (**Hinchliffe and Woodward, 2004**), to the kinds of social and political development that we can reasonably pursue.

Overstepping these limits, environmentalists claim, causes 'nature' to strike back at us in unforeseen ways. Consider the following examples. Climate change is no longer simply a naturally-driven phenomenon but is now influenced by the global warming resulting from the greenhouse gases produced by industrial societies. Human societies (or at least the industrialized ones) are, for the first time, producing their own climate, though in ways they did not intend and do not fully understand, with consequences we can do little better than guess at. Human reproduction is now being dramatically transformed by the advent and development of new reproductive technologies and the science of genetic engineering. If we can genetically re-engineer tomatoes and clone sheep, then what might we able to do to the human species in the not-too-distant future? What would such changes do to our sense of self and our identity as a single species? The development of genetic engineering and biotechnology is also radically transforming the 'natural' basis of agriculture, such that the reproduction of animals and plants is being industrialized via science in the large, commercial agri-businesses of the Western countries. Is genetically-modified food a new means of feeding an expanding world population or a long-term threat to human health? Finally, if economically viable solar power were to be developed (it's already a technical possibility), how might this change the economic fortunes of differing countries in a world where the access to and control of fossil fuels has been historically central to the development of industrial power?

FIGURE 3.3 Pollution incident on the River Kennet, Berkshire, which killed thousands of fish along a three mile stretch of river

The point of these examples is neither to encourage the technological pessimists nor the optimists but to suggest that, whatever happens in these and other fields (much of which we can't even begin to imagine at the moment), the effects are not only unpredictable for human societies but also for the natural world. What is novel about these kinds of development is that the risks (as well as the benefits) are now less localized, more consequential, potentially longer-term and less calculable than in the past. The paradox, in short, is that the more we know and the more we employ that knowledge in the search for local control, the more the general effects and consequences of our actions appear to escape our intentions. Our attempt to control the natural world reshapes it in unforeseen and unforeseeable ways. Nature ceases to be something that is external to society but becomes something that is, in crucial respects, shaped by society. The social and the natural come to interact with one another in complex ways, adding yet another layer of uncertainty to an already uncertain environment (see **Hinchliffe, 2004**). This kind of development leads to the idea that modern societies are characterized by risk.

SUMMARY

- Modern political ideologies incorporate a notion of progress based on scientific knowledge and the application of technology to produce economic growth.

- This notion of progress is questioned on the grounds that science may not be able to provide answers in complex and uncertain circumstances. The instrumental application of science in the service of controlling the natural environment may cause as many problems as it solves and there may be 'limits to growth'. These doubts have led to the formulation of the precautionary principle.

- There is a potential gap between the global nature of many environmental problems and the national organization of political units, namely nation-states, and of political decision making.

- A wider notion of our self-interest may be needed to cope with the idea that there are natural limits to what we can do socially and politically, and with the fact that the consequences of our attempts to control nature through social action constantly outrun our intentions as nature strikes back at us in unforeseen ways.

ACTIVITY 3.1

Think about some typical environmental issues, for example global warming; the extinction of natural species; radioactive pollution; traffic congestion; polluted rivers; concerns over genetically-modified crops; population growth; the consumption of non-renewable resources – and any others you can think of.

Now try to identify some of the ways in which these issues create problems for the conventional political ideologies of modern societies. Are these problems political, economic or cultural?

Use the first column of the table below to record your answers. You'll be asked to revisit this table and fill in the other columns as you progress through the chapter. By the end of this chapter, you should have created a table that provides you with a useful summary of the main points made in each section.

TABLE 3.1   Environmental problems for political ideologies

	Environmental problems of modern political ideologies	Responses of modern political ideologies	The challenge of green thinking	Green alternatives
Economics				
Politics				
Culture				

3 RESPONDING TO ENVIRONMENTAL PROBLEMS

Confronted with environmental problems, modern political ideologies have responded in different ways. We will see that they have all had important things to say about the environment. Green thinking as a general perspective is rooted in developments in the late nineteenth century. This means that although it has often been a minority current confined to the margins of political debate, green thinking has, in fact, been more or less coterminous with modern industrial development on a European and world scale. Modern political ideologies have been confronted with environmental problems for most of their history. In fact, what is novel is not so much the existence of environmental problems and green thinking but the ways in which green politics have moved centre-stage since the 1970s, such that all political ideologies now profess to be (at least pale) 'green'.

FIGURE 3.4 'Save our Downs' campaigners restoring ploughed area on site of special scientific interest (SSSI) chalk grasslands, Clayton to Offham escarpment, Sussex

3.1 Making the economy environmentally sustainable

One very common response to the kinds of environmental problems generated by economic activity is to argue that they could be resolved if we took a more enlightened view of our interests. According to this view, in order to address ecological concerns we have to recognize that not only are we part of nature, and that the pursuit of our economic interests has environmental implications, but that we also have an interest in the maintenance of certain kinds of environment for our own good. On this understanding, the central question is not one of a conflict between economic interests and environmental values but one between different kinds of human interests. And advice about how to reconcile conflicting interests is precisely what conventional political ideologies claim to offer.

ACTIVITY 3.2

The following reading is from the World Bank's, World Development Report, 1992: *Development and the Environment.* This is an example of the liberal, market-based approach to environmental problems and was much criticized by environmentalists when it appeared. The critics said that the World Bank's approach amounted to 'business as usual'. What do you think they meant by this?

After reading the extract, return to Table 3.1 on page 87 and fill in the 'Economics' box of the column headed 'Responses of modern political ideologies'.

READING 3.1

World Bank: 'Economic activity and the environment: key links'

This Report will argue that the adverse impact of economic growth on environmental degradation can be greatly reduced. Poor management of natural resources is already constraining development in some areas, and the growing scale of economic activity will pose serious challenges for environmental management. But rising incomes combined with sound environmental policies and institutions can form the basis for tackling both environmental and development problems. The key to growing sustainably is not to produce less but to produce differently. In some situations, such as protection of forests or control of emissions, good environmental policies may cause short-term growth to fall, even as welfare may rise. In other cases – for example, improved soil conservation practices or investments in water supply – the effect on output and incomes is likely to be positive. In still other areas the impacts are unclear. What is clear, however, is that failure to address environmental challenges will reduce the capacity for long-term development.

Understanding the problem

All economic activity involves transforming the natural world. Why does economic activity sometime lead to excessive environmental degradation? One reason is that many natural resources are shared and the true value of many environmental goods and services is not paid for by those who use them. Some natural resources are shared because there is no mechanism for enforcing property rights, as with frontier land, and others are shared because, as with the atmosphere, property rights are impossible to enforce. Unless an explicit agreement among users emerges, shared resources will be degraded over time, particularly as the scale of population and economic activity increases. In some cases government policies that subsidize environmental degradation can induce more damage than might otherwise occur. In other cases the poor, with few assets on which to draw, may have no choice but to excessively degrade natural resources.

The most pressing environmental problems are associated with resources that are regenerative but are undervalued and are therefore in danger of exhaustion. Air and water are renewable resources, but they have a finite capacity to assimilate emissions and wastes. If pollution exceeds this capacity, ecosystems can deteriorate rapidly. When fisheries or forests are excessively depleted to meet human needs, critical thresholds may be passed, resulting in the loss of ecosystems and species. Shortages of nonrenewable resources, such as metals, minerals, and energy, the possible exhaustion of which preoccupied early environmental debate, are of less concern. The evidence suggests that when the true value of such nonrenewable resources is reflected in the marketplace, there is no sign of excessive scarcity. (Box 1.4)

Water provides an example of an undervalued renewable resource that is showing signs of shortage. By the end of the 1990s six East African countries and all the North African countries will have annual renewable water supplies below the level at which societies generally experience water shortage. In China fifty cities face acute water shortages as groundwater levels drop 1 to 2 meters a year. In Mexico City groundwater is being pumped at rates 40 percent faster than natural re-charge. These shortages emerge when water is lost or wasted because its true scarcity value is not recognized. In such cities as Cairo, Jakarta, Lima, Manila, and Mexico City more than half of urban water supplies cannot be accounted for. In many countries scarce water is used for low-value agricultural crops, and farmers pay nothing for the water they use. The misuse of water in the Aral Sea in Central Asia is an extreme example of the failure to recognize the value of a natural resource.

Assessment of whether the regenerative capacity of a natural resource has been exceeded is complicated by uncertainty about the effect of economic activity on the environment. In the cases of soil erosion, atmospheric pollution, and loss of biodiversity, there is often substantial scientific uncertainty about the extent of environmental degradation. Controversy also surrounds the consequences of degradation. What are the health effects of certain pollutants? What will climate change do to the ecosystem? Can tropical forests be regenerated? The solutions are likewise often unclear. How quickly can the atmosphere restore itself? When will certain cleaner technologies become available and cost-effective? Uncertainty is an inherent part of environmental problems. To reduce it, decision makers need better information about environmental processes and social preferences.

BOX 1.4	**The dismal science – economics and scarcity of natural resources**

The debate about whether the world is running out of nonrenewable resources is as old as economics. The writings of Malthus and Ricardo, which predicted rapidly growing populations and increasing scarcity of resources, earned economics the name 'the dismal science'. For natural resources that are nonrenewable, increases in consumption necessarily imply a reduction in the available stock. The evidence, however, gives no support to the hypothesis that marketed nonrenewable resources such as metals, minerals, and energy are becoming scarcer in an economic sense. This is because potential or actual shortages are reflected in rising market prices, which in turn have induced new discoveries, improvements in efficiency, possibilities for substitution, and technological innovations.

The rise in the prices of energy and metals in the 1970s encouraged efficiency gains and substitutions that ultimately reduced the growth of demand. Examples of such technological changes include fiber optics, which replaced copper in telecommunications, the use of thinner coatings of tin, nickel, and zinc in a number of industries, the development of synthetic substitutes, and the recycling of aluminum and other materials. Similar efficiency gains were achieved in the energy sector. The use of metals and of energy per unit of output has declined steadily in industrial countries, although it is generally rising in developing countries. Current consumption as a proportion of reserves has declined for several mineral and energy resources (Box Table 1.4).

BOX TABLE 1.4 Energy and mineral reserves and consumption, 1970 and 1988

	Index of commercial reserves, 1988 (1970 = 100)	Annual consumption as a percentage of reserves	
		1970	1988
Energy resources			
Crude oil	163	2.7	2.2
Gas	265	2.1	1.5
Mineral resources			
Bauxite	373	0.2	0.1
Copper	131	2.6	3.1
Iron ore	74	0.5	0.8
Lead	75	4.7	8.1
Nickel	72	0.8	1.7
Tin	150	5.4	3.7
Zinc	176	0.3	0.2

Source: World Bank data

Declining price trends also indicate that many nonrenewables have become more, rather than less, abundant (Box Figure 1.4).

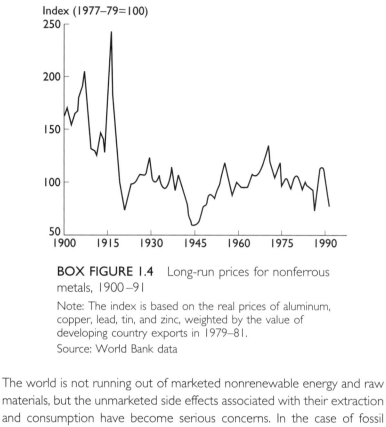

BOX FIGURE 1.4   Long-run prices for nonferrous metals, 1900–91

Note: The index is based on the real prices of aluminum, copper, lead, tin, and zinc, weighted by the value of developing country exports in 1979–81.

Source: World Bank data

The world is not running out of marketed nonrenewable energy and raw materials, but the unmarketed side effects associated with their extraction and consumption have become serious concerns. In the case of fossil fuels, the real issue is not a potential shortage but the environmental effects associated with their use, particularly local air pollution and carbon dioxide emissions. Similarly, the problems with minerals extraction are pollution and destruction of natural habitat. Because 95 percent of the total material removed from the earth is waste that often contain heavy metals such as copper, iron, tin, and mercury, these commonly find their way into rivers, groundwater, and soils.

Source: World Bank, 1992

C O M M E N T

I think there are perhaps three ways in which the World Bank's approach might be described as 'business as usual'. Firstly, the Report says that: 'The key to growing sustainability is not to produce less but to produce differently'. The Report does not see either present levels of economic production and consumption or the continued pursuit of economic growth as problematic. Secondly, the Report argues that 'the true value of many environmental goods and services is not paid for by those who use them', either because of the absence of property rights in their use (see **Himmelweit and Simonetti, 2004**) or through the existence of distorted (e.g. subsidized) prices. It recommends using the market mechanism to allocate environmental resources efficiently, just like other commodities in a free market. This argument is illustrated by the contrast drawn between regenerative resources that are not properly valued (e.g. air, water, fish stocks) and which constitute a serious problem, and non-renewable resources (e.g. fossil fuel, metals, minerals) that are properly valued, where 'there is no sign of excessive scarcity', where 'the world is not running out of marketed nonrenewable energy and raw materials'. And thirdly, the Report recognizes that the assessment of environmental problems 'is complicated by uncertainty about the effect of economic activity on the environment', and says that the response to this is to seek 'better information'.

The World Bank's approach is a good example of the way that liberal thinkers approach environmental problems produced by economic activity. They argue that many environmental problems arise because certain interests are not recognized as they are not incorporated into the market framework of economic activity. This is because environmental resources are either not subject to clearly defined and enforceable property rights or do not have a price, or both. Who owns the atmosphere or the oceans? What is the price of a whale or a rainforest? Since the market can only function efficiently when resources are owned and priced, in the case of many environmental resources, the market fails. The liberal solution is to establish ownership rights and prices and then to allow the market to operate. Liberals are aware that in some cases it may be very difficult or impossible to establish property rights and prices, and in those cases public action through the agency of the state may be called for. But the general idea is that the self-interest which drives the market can be harnessed to environmentally benign ends to the extent that environmental resources are owned and priced like other commodities. This free market or liberal environmentalism has had a major impact in shaping public policy both within liberal-democratic capitalist states and in the wider international arena.

Social democratic and conservative thinkers are more sceptical about the feasibility and desirability of market-based solutions to environmental problems. In particular, they raise objections to each of the three elements of the liberal approach identified above. Firstly, how can the interests of those who cannot participate in the market be addressed? The most obvious instance of this point is the status of future generations. Clearly, future generations cannot trade in the market with the current generation. Assuming that the present generation wants to pass on an inhabitable environment to its descendants, how can these future interests be registered in the market now? Secondly, is it appropriate that monetary value should be the sole measure of environmental value? Certainly, you can ask people how much they would be willing to pay, say, to see whales left free from commercial use, or estimate the value of a mountain such as Snowdon to walkers by reckoning the price

FIGURE 3.5 Whale and Greenpeace inflatable dinghy with two activists on board being hauled up the stern ramp of a Japanese whaling ship, which is violating UN convention articles, in the Southern Ocean Sanctuary

of its alternative use as farmland. But are these the appropriate ways of deciding whether to resume commercial whaling or to ascertain the price the National Trust should pay for Snowdon? Thirdly, in the presence of real uncertainty about the environmental effects of economic activity, is it enough to call for more information? What if further information is not available for some reason? Perhaps we need to reverse the burden of proof and assume that economic activity *is* environmentally harmful unless it can be shown to be otherwise, rather than assuming that economic growth is good unless it can be shown to have unacceptable environmental costs. This is the idea behind the 'precautionary principle'.

Social democratic and conservative thinkers argue that it is not appropriate to leave such questions to the market; environmental problems are not simply examples of market failure or the inefficient provision of public goods. Critics of the individualistic bias of liberal theory argue that many, if not all, environmental goods are inherently social; they involve questions of the public good; they are irreducibly questions of collective choice and therefore belong to the realm of politics, not economics. That is to say, if environmental resources cannot or should not be owned and valued, then an alternative decision-making mechanism to the market is needed.

At this point, however, social democracy and conservatism tend to part company. As an alternative to the market, social democracy favours democracy. On this view, environmental goods should be decided on the basis of the discussion of values in the public sphere. Does democratic decision making within the institutional framework of liberal democracy provide a satisfactory alternative or complement to the market? Broadly speaking, social democratic thinkers are confident that it does. They argue that if people think about their interests in an enlightened manner and are able to debate these openly with one another, they will come to see that various trade-offs between economic and environmental interests, between the rich and the poor, and between present and future generations are in the collective interest of all.

The conservative tradition is sceptical of both the market and democracy, since both presuppose that we know what we are doing. Conservative ideology has been described as a 'politics of imperfection' (Quinton, 1978). This means many different things, but one central idea is that we can have only a very limited understanding of our place in the world and the consequences of our actions. For this reason, conservatism, as its name suggests, is a reactive ideology; it defines itself in opposition to the proposals of other ideologies and seeks to conserve what we already have. It is suspicious of change and seeks to defend what is 'traditional' and 'natural'. This gives conservatism a bias against interfering in the natural environment, whether through the market or by democratically agreed public policy.

Feminist thinking on the environment is very diverse. Some feminist thinking has borrowed from other ideologies and seeks to incorporate a concern with gender and racialized patriarchal power relations into the ideological debate. That is to say, feminism challenges the assumption of modern political ideologies that only the male-dominated public sphere is what really matters. In these cases, feminist views on the environment mirror those of the relevant ideology. For example, liberal feminism takes a liberal position on environmental problems, while emphasizing those aspects of women's lives that are specifically affected. However, there is also a more thorough-going feminist critique of modern political ideologies which goes beyond raising concerns specific to women's interests. Radical feminism offers a very different perspective to all the other established ideologies and it forms an important component of green thinking in the form of 'eco-feminism'. We consider this position in more detail in Section 4.3.

3.2   Environmental globalization and the politics of the nation-state

We noted in Section 2 that environmental problems are very often global in one sense or another, that is, they involve some combination of cross-border patterns of cause and effect (e.g. various forms of pollution from nuclear radiation to acid rain); environmental interdependence between one country and another (e.g. the connections between poverty, population growth and the pressure on resources, or the complex web of cause and effect involved in global warming and climate change); and threats to the environmental integrity of the global commons (e.g. the pollution of the atmosphere and the oceans). Political decision making, by contrast, is national in scope and the repository of legitimate power in the modern world, that is, the primary source of authority, is the territorially-bounded, sovereign nation-state (**McGrew, 2004**).

How are questions that cut across separate political jurisdictions to be addressed? To what extent can frameworks and solutions appropriate to the national level be transferred to the international or global arena? When we turn to these global dimensions of environmental problems, the issues are posed starkly. The necessary public functions that are required either to constitute and regulate markets or to supplement market mechanisms with democratically formulated public action all assume the presence of a reasonably legitimate and hence effective agency of extracting resources and enforcing rules – namely, the state. But as Todd Sandler (1997, p.13) rightly points out: 'Nations are loathe to empower a supranational body with the authority to collect taxes, to regulate transnational externalities, to provide international public goods, to assign property rights, or to redistribute income'. And, of course, many international environmental problems do take the form of transnational externalities arising from environmental interdependence, or the inadequate provision of global public goods, or the degradation of the global commons because of collective action problems. But, given the absence of a global political authority, how are co-ordinated resource allocation decisions to be made when there is no authority to impose either command and control solutions or to implement economic instruments such as taxes and quotas?

For those environmental problems which may be treated as cases of market failure, that is, where the problem may be considered as one of externalities or as the inadequate provision of public goods, liberal and social democratic ideologies may have some answers. Some environmental problems take the form of externalities which cross borders in an identifiable direction: that is, they arise where economic activity in one state inflicts harm upon another. For example, the Chernobyl nuclear accident in the Ukraine inflicted harm on many countries in the European Union. In a case like this, if we assume that the damage to the countries affected is greater than the benefits to the Ukraine (cheap nuclear power!), that is, if we assume that the level of pollution is not optimal, then there are potential gains from co-operation between the Ukraine and the other states involved.

However, bargaining to achieve this outcome may be difficult if the states assess the costs and benefits involved differently (and given that the parties are separate sovereign states this is more than likely), especially if they behave in a self-interested way in disclosing information to one another. Moreover, the bargaining process among more than two states may be complicated by the problem of free-riding, by one state seeking to benefit from the agreement between the others while not itself co-operating. The position is further compounded by the fact that in international law, the rights that sovereign states can enforce against one another are very limited compared with the rights that private property owners have in relation to one another within a given state. This means that, in general, the polluter has no incentive to desist unless compensated by the polluted, and so the necessary payments will generally have to involve the victim-pays principle rather than the widely supported notion that the polluter should pay. In the example above, this would mean that instead of the Ukraine compensating countries for the radioactive damage caused, other European states would have to pay the Ukraine to improve the safety of its nuclear reactors (which, in fact, the EU did because they valued a radioactive-free environment).

In the case of reciprocal externalities, where all the states involved are both polluters and polluted, the distribution of environmental 'bads' will be shared. For example, coal-burning power stations in the UK release gases into the atmosphere which combine with rainfall to produce 'acid rain' that falls and damages forests in Britain, Scandinavia and Germany; likewise power stations in Germany and Scandinavia burn coal, etc. The adverse effects of climate change resulting from global warming is another good example of this kind of shared problem. (Of course, the net position of countries will differ, some states will be more sinned against than sinners.) In these cases, it will be in the interests of the states concerned acting separately to undertake some reduction of pollution. But in the absence of co-operation, the level achieved will be inadequate, less than each would want if they could be sure that the others would co-operate. The relative distribution of costs and benefits between the states affected will influence their ability to make co-operative agreements. Nevertheless, states will have a purely national interest in co-operating to some extent. In these cases, co-operative norms and agreements can be self-sustaining, given sufficient common knowledge of the problem, repeated interaction with the other states concerned, the ability to monitor the behaviour of others and the power to enforce sanctions against them. The relatively successful international convention to reduce ozone-depleting chemicals is one important example.

Thus, even in the absence of a centralized world authority, externalities can be somewhat corrected and global public goods may still be provided if the circumstances and the incentives are right. Inter-state co-operation may thus be motivated by efficiency gains as well as benefiting from economies of scale and scope in the provision and management of public goods. These considerations suggest that international co-operation for environmental improvement may be possible even given the absence of enforcement mechanisms beyond the realm of the sovereign nation-state. This kind of analysis underpins the international aspects of much Northern thinking.

However, it is important to emphasize that markets and property rights depend on mechanisms of enforcement in order to function. And where the enforcement is carried out by separate sovereign states, indeed where, very often, the creation of the markets and the property rights has to be done by states, then the valuation of costs and benefits and the definition of private property rights may well conflict. As we have seen, bargaining may overcome these problems, but the scope for imperfect outcomes is considerably greater at the international level given this absence of an overarching mechanism of calculation and enforcement.

Precisely because the system of separate sovereign states is likely to produce less than satisfactory outcomes to global environmental problems, even when those states are able to achieve a degree of international co-operation, an alternative response to the challenge posed by environmental globalization is to look beyond the nation-state, to seek for a supra-national form of political authority, and thereby constitute legitimate public power on the same dimensions as the problems it aims to deal with. If the scope of the problem is global, then why not the scope of the authority charged with dealing with it? The need for this kind of thinking is often pressed by those who maintain that if states cannot maintain a degree of environmental security for their populations under the current arrangements of national sovereignty, then this will likely call into question the legitimacy of the sovereign state as its performance is progressively undermined in a crucial area.

It is certainly possible to design and implement international agreements between states to cope with environmental problems. It is also possible to use market-based mechanisms in dealings between sovereign states (marketable permits in carbon dioxide emissions to deal with greenhouse gases are an important example) but there are serious questions as to how far this approach can be developed. As we have seen, the basic problems stem, on the one hand, from the difficulty of negotiating and agreeing costs and benefits when the arbiters of those costs and benefits are separate sovereign states behaving strategically, and on the other, from the fact that states have rights in their own territory (and in their corresponding territorial waters and airspace) but relatively few (and often prohibitively expensive) means of monitoring or enforcing those rights. This leads some to argue that the only way around these problems is to constrain the sovereign preferences of states. One obvious forum for such activity is the United Nations, and one principle that might guide such deliberations is some form of democratic representation at that level – rather than the current bargaining based on the distribution of power among states. At the moment these ideas are little more than aspirations, but it is clear that conceptualizing and implementing change of this kind would involve a fundamental rethinking of a politics based on the nationally-bounded territorial state.

ACTIVITY 3.3

Return to Table 3.1 on page 87 and fill in the 'Politics' box of the column headed 'Responses of modern political ideologies'.

3.3   Enlightened self-interest?

We saw in Section 3.1 that a concern with the natural capacities and needs of humans, and the associated idea that there might be natural limits to certain forms of development, can be squared with the standard concerns of political ideologies. As the political theorist Tim Hayward has noted: 'most coherent theories of the good life ought to be able to accommodate the fact of natural capacities and needs; and theories of justice ought in principle to be able to extend their traditional concern with conditions of scarcity to include the idea of natural limits' (1998, p.11). Where environmental politics poses a more difficult and far-reaching challenge to modern political debate is the suggestion that the non-human world (both inanimate nature and other species, as well as the relations between these) constitutes a source of value and interest in its own right, independently of the existence of human beings.

The idea here is that nature cannot and should not be used merely instrumentally for the benefit of humans. This radical view that non-human nature constitutes a source of independent value has two strands:

1   the idea that there is an intrinsic value to non-human nature

2   the notion that we should reject what is termed an anthropocentric (or human-centred) view of the world.

We will see that taking these ideas seriously poses a very substantial challenge to traditional thinking about the representation, protection and advancement of values, interests and rights, since if non-human nature constitutes a source of value and can be said to have interests and rights, then how are these to be defined and realized?

ACTIVITY 3.4

Return to Table 3.1 on page 87 and fill in the 'Culture' box of the column headed 'Responses of modern political ideologies'.

SUMMARY

- We have identified two main strategies for dealing with the potential gap between global environmental problems and the national scope of politics: firstly, seek international co-operation on the basis of the enlightened self-interest of sovereign national states; secondly, seek to reconstitute political authority and action at a global level through a reform of the United Nations system.

- Liberalism has responded by a strategy of 'business as usual' and tries to incorporate environmental interests and values into the decision making of the market.

- Social democracy builds upon the liberal approach but seeks a greater role for democratic decision making in the public sphere.

- Conservatism urges us to conserve the nature and tradition that we already have and is sceptical about change to the environment.

- Socialism urged us to plan our control of the natural world on the basis of science.

- Some feminist thinking offers a potentially radical alternative to all of these ways of dealing with the environment.

4 THE CHALLENGE OF GREEN THINKING

Consider the following brief extract from Jonathan Porritt's book *Seeing Green* (1984). Porritt is a prominent green thinker in Britain and a former director of Friends of the Earth.

> The politics of the Industrial Age, left, right and centre, is like a three-lane motorway, with different vehicles in different lanes, but *all* heading in the same direction. ... It is [the green] perception that the motorway of industrialism inevitably leads to the abyss ... there must be something with which we can replace it; not another super-ideology (for ideologies are themselves part of the problem), *but a different world view.* ...
>
> [G]reen politics is not just another dimension of the disintegrating industrial world order; it is something qualitatively different. ... the politics of radical ecology embraces *every* dimension of human experience and *all* life on Earth – that is to say, it goes a great deal further in terms of political comprehensiveness than any other political persuasion or ideology has ever gone before. ...
>
> Everything that once served to enhance both individual and collective security now serves to undermine it: ... the maximization of production and consumption, higher productivity, increased GNP, the industrialization of the Third World, expanded world trade, the comprehensive exploitation of the Earth's resources, an emphasis on individualism, the triumph of materialism, the sovereignty of the nation-state, uncontrolled technological development – these were once the hallmarks of success, the guarantors of security. Collectively they now threaten our very survival. ...
>
> The spirit of industrialism is rapidly losing its grip. The doctrine of scientific rationality and material growth has signally failed to provide people with any lasting ideals or values – so much so that the very legitimacy of the dominant world order is now in question.
>
> (Porritt, 1984, pp.43–4, 215–8)

Ecologism
Ecologism is the complex set of ideas that seeks to put the relations between human beings and the rest of the natural environment at the centre of our thinking.

Porritt is an advocate for green thinking and his book paints a sharp contrast between the concerns of green thinking, or what is often called **ecologism**, on the one side, and the priorities of the modern political ideologies, on the other. According to Porritt, all modern political ideologies are committed to a materialistic notion of progress as unlimited economic growth and consumption, to a politics based on the nation-state, and to values of individualism and scientific rationality. Green politics, by contrast, includes such things as 'a reverence for the Earth and all its creatures'; social justice among all the people in the world – rich and poor, North and South – as well as between current and future generations; a rejection of materialism, industrialism and instrumental rationality; the protection of the environment;

personal growth and spiritual development; participatory democracy; and 'self-reliance and decentralized communities'. However, green politics is not about a return to the past, 'harking back to some pre-industrial Golden Age', since the past 'wasn't golden' and industrialism 'brought enormous benefits to millions of people, in terms of both material improvements and democratic rights' (Porritt, 1984, p.19). Rather, green politics insists that we must now enter a post-industrial age, where we can no longer trade-off economic growth against environmental concerns, nor the interests of the rich and the North against those of the poor and the South, nor the interests of the present against the future, nor the interests of humans against those of other species. The industrial era, the nation-state, scientific rationalism, and the political ideologies associated with these, have had their day.

FIGURE 3.6   Dr Caroline Lucas, Green MEP

As the brief extract from Porritt's book above suggests, green thinking has a distinct perspective on the place of the human species within the natural world, and what he refers to as 'the politics of radical ecology' (p.216) is a set of ethical and political ideals deriving from this perspective. In this section we seek to explore ecology or ecologism in a little more detail by examining its origins, the kinds of challenges it poses to modern political ideologies, and some of the complex ways in which it appeals to 'nature'.

ACTIVITY 3.5

Before reading any further, try to make some entries in the 'Economics', 'Politics' and 'Culture' boxes in the column headed 'The challenge of green thinking', in Table 3.1 on page 87. If you are stuck for ideas, re-read the passage from Porritt above.

4.1   The origins of ecologism

The theory of ecology and the term 'ecologism' have their origins in late nineteenth century Europe. The term ecology (*Oekologie*) was coined by a German biologist, Ernst Haeckel (1834–1919) to refer to 'the science of relations between organisms and their environment'. The discipline of ecology was thus the study of organisms; their characteristics, especially their life-cycles; their environments, in particular the kinds of environment in which they flourished; and their place in the totality of all organisms and environments, the totality being understood as connected and related to one another through flows of resources and energy. In addition to its biological beginnings, there were two other important connotations of 'ecology' as it was originally used and which continue to be important today. The first connection was between '*oekologie*' and the idea of a careful use of economic resources to sustain the moral and material well-being of the community. The second linkage was between 'ecology' and 'ethology', the latter being the science of animal (including human) behaviour.

Although Haeckel did not develop all the implications of these ideas, he played a leading role in founding not only ecology as a science but also ecologism as a political ideology. Anna Bramwell, a historian of ecological thought in the twentieth century, has argued that Haeckel was an ecologist in three important ways:

> Firstly, he saw the universe as a unified and balanced organism. Space and organic beings were made of the same atoms. ... He also believed that man and animals had the same moral and natural status ... Thirdly, he preached the doctrine that nature was the source of truth and wise guidance about man's life. Human society should be re-organized along the lines suggested by scientific observation of the natural world. Through his influence, he enabled ecologism to become a viable political creed.
>
> (Bramwell, 1989, p.43)

Around the same time that Haeckel was beginning to elaborate a distinctive ecological perspective from within biology, others (known as 'energy economists') were trying to come to terms with the implications of the findings of modern physics about matter and energy for economic arrangements. These ideas suggested, in the words of a later energy economist, Kenneth Boulding (1966), that we cannot pretend to live in a 'cowboy economy', that is, one where there is a limitless frontier which we can extend in search of new resources, but rather we must learn to cope with the almost closed system of 'Spaceship Earth', where the only truly external source of energy is solar power. Today, many of us take the finite nature of useable resources for granted, but when these ideas first spread outside the academic world of theoretical physics into the wider culture they had a profound impact.

In order to see the potentially far-reaching implications of these considerations, we need to look at the notion of 'efficiency' in conventional economic thinking. One of the achievements of nineteenth century social thought was an apparently successful defence of the status of the new economics to be a science. The liberal economics of competitive markets in a monetary economy claimed to discover a value-free notion of 'efficiency', a standard against which alternative social arrangements could be judged. But it soon became apparent that if one thought about the concept of 'efficiency' in energy terms one would reach very different conclusions than if one approached the issue economically.

For example, while large-scale, mechanized, chemically-assisted agriculture produced much greater output per unit of monetary input than small-scale peasant production, when measured by units of energy used to produce a given quantity of food (itself a form of energy supply), peasant agriculture was superior or more 'efficient' in energy terms. Similar conclusions can be arrived at by considering accounts drawn up in terms of another scarce resource – time. Calculations of time budgets, that is, the allocation of time between different uses, show that the economics of time is not the same as the economics of money. Take the example of transport as developed by Ivan Illich in the 1970s, in which he contrasted transport in the United States and a peasant society:

> The typical American male devotes more than 1,600 hours a year to his car. He sits in it while it goes and while it stands idling. He parks it and searches for it. He earns the money to put down on it and to meet the monthly instalments. He works to pay for petrol, tolls, insurance, taxes and tickets. He spends four of his sixteen waking hours on the road or gathering his resources for it. The model American puts in 1,600 hours to get 7,500 miles: less than five miles per hour. In countries deprived of a transportation industry, people manage to do the same, walking wherever they want to go, and they allocate only three to eight per cent of their society's time budget to traffic instead of 28 per cent.
>
> (Illich, 1973, p.30; quoted in Porritt, 1984, p.122)

What is more, in our big cities we don't get to travel much faster than a peasant does: the average speed of traffic in London in 2003 was about eleven miles per hour as it had been throughout the 1990s, about the same as a horse and cart in the 1890s.

In other words, what is economically efficient is not necessarily the same as what is efficient when calculated in terms of energy use or in terms of our time. And if useable energy is in finite supply, as our time certainly is, then why should society opt for the economist's notion of efficiency over that of the ecologist's? From an ecological point of view, then, the notion of efficiency developed in economic theory is not value-neutral but, instead, reflects a notion of efficiency *within* an economic and monetary sphere, a sphere that is itself but part of a wider system bounded by the ultimate constraints of energy and time.

Perhaps because of these somewhat obscure origins in the natural sciences, ecologism developed in isolation from the dominant political ideologies of the twentieth century. Indeed, it was only in the 1970s that its two strands, the moral and cultural critique of a human-centred and instrumental attitude towards the natural world and the empirical and quantitative critique of monetary economics, fused again into a powerful political movement. As a distinctive political ideology and movement, green politics is comparatively recent, though we should not overlook earlier flowerings of ecological concern in the 1930s, 1950s and 1960s.

4.2 Radical environmentalism

We saw above that ecological thinking seeks to challenge the instrumental use of the natural world by and for human beings. But of what would a non-instrumental attitude to nature consist? What does it mean to say that there is an intrinsic value to non-human nature and what does a rejection of **anthropocentrism** entail? Many ecological thinkers are not convinced by the attempts of the modern political ideologies to deal with these questions. Let us begin with an example. We saw above that liberals and social democrats argued that a combination of markets and democracy can solve environmental problems. But how does democratic decision making solve the problem of meeting the interests of those that cannot participate in debate? Other animal species, forests and the not-yet-born are not and cannot be part of our democratic process, any more than they can be participants in the market. They can only enter the democratic process when their interests are represented by others, an inherently paternalistic position. Surely this is just a form of instrumentalism at one remove. Animals, plants or future generations will be valued and accorded consideration only in so far as it suits those who are participants in the debate to do so. If we don't care about them, and if we value the future less than the present (because we won't live for ever), then their prospects for survival may be very bleak. It is at this point that ecologism's concern for the intrinsic value of non-human nature and its rejection of anthropocentrism become very important.

Anthropocentrism
Literally a 'human-centred' approach. The idea that human beings are at the centre of the world or universe. An outlook which considers things from the viewpoint of human beings.

FIGURE 3.7   Radical protest

The notion of 'intrinsic value' and the injunction to reject 'anthropocentrism' are difficult ideas and we need to unpack them a little bit to see where the ecological argument is going. Let us consider the idea of intrinsic value first.

The intuition here is relatively simple: namely, that non-human nature has value that is independent of human beings and their concerns. At this point it may be helpful to distinguish between the physical environment and the living, biological realm. It might also be useful to distinguish within the living realm between plants and animals and perhaps between different kinds of species within the animal kingdom. We can then ask whether the notion of an intrinsic value to non-human nature is meant to apply to all of the natural world or merely to the living, or even just to some parts of the living world. Should we value the HIV virus which causes AIDS in the same way that we might value, say, the tiger? This is important since the radical ecological injunction is to respect and preserve the intrinsic value of non-human nature. Clearly, it is part of the nature of human beings, like that of other species, to interact with the rest of the natural world. It follows directly that the idea of complete non-interference in the affairs of other species and ecosystems is incoherent, since it would involve a denial of *our* nature. Human beings, by their very nature, act in and have effects on the natural world – as do all other species.

Now consider the following examples. Does it make sense to say that there is an intrinsic value to, say, crude oil and that crude oil has interests that ought to be respected? Most of us would answer 'no'. It might be sensible for us to conserve crude oil for future generations or to burn less of it and thus release less carbon dioxide into the atmosphere, thereby limiting our additions to the greenhouse gases which cause global warming and climate change, but it is difficult to see how we can do anything other than take a (hopefully enlightened) instrumental attitude to the use of crude oil. But what about whales, tigers and future generations? Surely, in these cases, we can identify something very closely akin to our 'common-sense' notion of interests, one which allows them to flourish, and an inclination to respect such interests as ends in themselves and not just as means to our ends.

On what basis, then, might we accord the same kind of respect to other animals as we grant to one another (and to future generations)? This is a deep and difficult question reaching very far into the justifications of why we accord respect to one another in the first place. But you might like to think about your answer to the following question put by Tim Hayward: 'Why should we restrict respect to beings capable of rational freedom [i.e. one another, humans] rather than extend it to any beings with powers whose exercise can be enhanced or thwarted by the actions of we agents?' (1998, p.137). Hayward's own answer is as follows: 'Unless rationality were to be seen as apart from nature (indeed, as somehow 'above' the rest of nature, and not just as a ... level within the totality of nature), then there could be no reason I can think of'. If your conclusion is similar to Hayward's, at least for some species (remember the HIV virus!), then you are no longer operating with an instrumental attitude towards nature, you are according intrinsic value to at least some other parts of the natural world.

In moving beyond an instrumental attitude towards nature has one also overcome anthropocentrism? Remember that the term means 'human-centredness'. What does it mean to overcome or go beyond a human-centred approach? Once again, a little unpacking might make things clearer. Anthropocentrism might be understood in a cosmological sense to refer to the view that human beings are the centre of the world or universe, the 'measure of all things'. Overcoming anthropocentrism would thus amount to taking the view that human beings are but one part of a wider natural order, one part of nature. We could come to see this either scientifically or spiritually, or both, since the findings of modern science undermine the pretensions of humanity to any cosmic centrality just as firmly as any system of religious belief.

Biocentrism
Literally, centred on the biological world. Contrasted with anthropocentrism, biocentrism involves taking the standpoint of all living things.

Ecocentrism
As with biocentrism, a contrast to anthropocentrism, but now taking the standpoint of the environment as a whole, including both animate and inanimate matter.

However, anthropocentrism can also be understood as an ethical and political viewpoint. In this case, the relevant contrasts are with **biocentrism** and **ecocentrism**. If anthropocentrism means that one's moral outlook is centred on the consideration and respect due to human beings, then biocentrism involves giving moral consideration to all living beings and ecocentrism means respecting whole ecosystems, including the non-living parts of nature. In the case of a biocentric perspective, we have already seen in our discussion of intrinsic values that there may be grounds for respecting the interests of non-human life forms. If we accept the notion of such values we can seek to avoid and overcome what has been called 'speciesism', the arbitrary discrimination on the basis of species. To that extent it is at least an intelligible position to combine anthropocentrism and biocentrism, though it is still human beings who are according value and attributing and respecting interests.

An ecocentric perspective, by contrast, would seek not only to respect other living beings but to accord value to whole ecosystems, including their non-living parts. But by what criteria are different ecosystems to be judged, if not by reference back to anthropocentric and biocentric ones? (Remember, human beings, like other species, cannot avoid interacting with and changing their ecosystems.)

My answer would be this. We can certainly reject anthropocentrism in its cosmological meaning and ethically we can accord value and respect to other living beings. But what would seem to be inescapable is that it is still human beings who are doing the valuing and, moreover, that where we have to judge and evaluate whole ecosystems, we can only do so by reference back to the interests of humans and other species. (We can seek to respect the interests of other animals, or protect the rainforests, that is, we can try to care for and preserve the conditions of their flourishing, but we cannot ask animals what their interests are, nor can the rainforests tell us under what conditions they will flourish.) Ethically speaking, a degree of anthropocentrism seems to be inevitable.

ACTIVITY 3.6

The following reading is from David Arnold's book, *The Problem of Nature*.
What do you think it is saying about the representation and conceptualization
of nature?

READING 3.2

David Arnold: 'Environment, culture and European expansion'

The environmentalist paradigm provides us with a distinctive model for
understanding and explaining the human past. It does not represent nature in
the abstract, as an eco-system apart from, or devoid of, human influence and
intelligence. On the contrary, it is frankly anthropocentric, seeing in nature a
reflection or a cause of the human condition, whether physical, social or moral. It
arises from a widely held and historically enduring belief that a significant
relationship exists between what is conventionally referred to (even in
these gender-conscious times) as 'man' and 'nature', and that this
relationship influences the character of individual societies and the course of
their histories.

Historically, of course, there has been no consensus as to how this influence
might operate. In some instances, it is seen to be so strictly determinist as to
allow little room for human free will. The environment, typically in the form of
climate and topography, but sometimes also of disease or other 'natural'
hazards, dictates the physical and mental characteristics of a society, its modes
of subsistence, its cultural life and political institutions. It even determines
whether a society is able to scale the heights of civilization or is confined to
the depths of savagery and barbarism. Other writers, less given to extremes,
have preferred a 'possibilist' position: the physical environment restricts human
societies in some ways but not in others, or only does so in the more primitive
stages of human development. The more mature and civilized a society
becomes, the less it lies in nature's thrall; indeed, the mark of a civilization is
precisely its ability to rise above narrow environmental constraints. At
other times, and increasingly in recent decades, the basic paradigm has been
reversed: mankind has won mastery over nature, it is argued, but has abused and
mistreated it, and now must live with the environmental and social
consequences of its Promethean act. This kind of environmentalism tends to
concentrate on the harm humans have done to the environment (and hence to
themselves) through industrial pollution, mechanized farming, the destruction of
forests, and the extinction of animal and plant species.

The environmentalist paradigm thus covers a wide range of interpretative
options: from history as the harmonious working together of people and
nature, at one extreme, to an irreversible ecological crisis precipitated
by human greed and folly, at the other. But what is common to all these
views is a belief that nature and culture are dynamically linked and that
history is in some central way connected with this intimate and continuing
relationship.

It is, however, worth reflecting how diversely different ages and societies have understood this environmentalist idea. For instance, barely two hundred years ago it was not uncommon in Western society to stress the harmful influences of the environment, one in which disease-bearing 'miasmas' or 'foul exhalations' were believed to issue from almost every possible source – from marshes and swamps, from river banks, forests and dense undergrowth, as well as from human habitations. Although the term as such was not then used, environmentalism at that time signified an awareness of the hazards of nature and the need, for the sake of one's health, to avoid them as much as possible or to destroy the source of the miasmas by draining marshes and clearing jungles. Today, Western attitudes have been substantially reversed. The 'natural' environment is seen to be intrinsically healthy. It is we who make it unhealthy by our abuse of it or endanger our health by interfering with nature.

Source: Arnold, 1996

COMMENT

My answer would be something like this. In thinking about the environment, we represent and interpret nature in human terms, we project human qualities onto the natural world. Arnold says that the 'environmentalist paradigm' is 'frankly anthropocentric' (anthropocentric = human-centred). We do this because we believe there are close connections between 'man' and 'nature'. However, the essential character of the connections between human society and the natural world can be and have been conceived in very different ways. Firstly, nature can be seen as shaping or determining society; secondly, nature can be seen as setting limits to the kinds of society that are possible; and thirdly, society can be seen as controlling and thus shaping nature. The latter idea, Arnold says, is distinctively modern. Finally, Arnold draws attention to the varied ways in which nature has been *evaluated* by human societies. In particular, he draws a contrast between a traditional view of nature as harmful and threatening, as something which must be tamed and controlled by human society, and a more recent view, which may in fact be a reinvention of an older spiritual view (though Arnold does not say this), in which nature is seen as benign and naturally good, something to be preserved and cared for.

4.3 What is nature?

Much of the force of the green challenge to modern political ideologies derives from the powerful idea that human societies should not and ultimately cannot treat the natural world as a mere instrument, a resource to be used as humans see fit. As the philosopher Kate Soper has pointed out:

> [Nature] has come to occupy a central place on the political agenda as a result of
> ecological crisis, where it figures as a general concept through which we are asked
> to re-think our current use of resources, our relations to other forms of life, and
> our place within, and responsibilities towards the eco-system.
>
> (Soper, 1995, p.2)

Green thinking encourages us to preserve and protect nature, to live in
harmony with nature and to recognize our own limited place within the
natural order. But what do we mean by 'nature'? Raymond Williams famously
observed that 'nature [is] perhaps the most complex word in the [English]
language' (1976, p.219). What he meant by this was not only that 'nature' has
a variety of different meanings and that it has been used in different ways in
different historical contexts but also that what is taken to be natural almost
always involves a degree of projecting socially defined attributes onto the
natural world. In one sense this is perhaps inevitable, since we can only
know nature under some particular description and conceptualization or
another. We cannot have unmediated knowledge of the natural world, and
the descriptions and conceptualizations we use to talk about nature often
encode particular socially generated attitudes and interests, whether these be
scientific, spiritual or evaluative (**Hinchliffe, 2004**).

In addition to these different uses of the word 'nature', the scope of the term
is also very variable. Probably the commonest usage of nature is to designate
that part of the material world which human beings have not played a part in
making, the natural is the not-human, as when we speak of the natural
environment. A wider, cosmological sense of nature, however, refers to 'that
totality of being of which we in some sense conceive ourselves as forming a
part' (Soper, 1995, p.21). The ways in which human beings have conceived
their place within nature in this sense changed dramatically with the
secularization of society, and the apparent revival of new forms of spirituality
may be changing these conceptions yet again (see Chapter 2).

Then there is the vexed question of 'human nature'. This idea is often
invoked to differentiate us from other species when it is said that we are, by
nature, 'rational' or 'social', but equally the notion of human nature can be
used to express our place in the animal world and our fixed natural
properties. The word 'nature', then, is complex and we need to attend
carefully to its use in particular contexts. In short, there is nothing natural
about 'nature'.

We can explore this point a little further and illustrate it by considering one
particular element of green thinking, namely the contribution of 'eco-
feminism'. In her book *Staying Alive,* Vandana Shiva writes as follows:

> The recovery of the feminine principle is an intellectual and political challenge to
> maldevelopment as a patriarchal project of domination and destruction, of
> violence and subjugation, of dispossession and the dispensability of both
> women and nature. The politics of life centred on the feminine principle

challenges fundamental assumptions not just in political economy, but also in the science of life-threatening processes. ...

The reductionist and universalising tendencies of such 'science' become inherently violent and destructive in a world which is inherently related and diverse. The feminine principle becomes an oppositional category of non-violent ways of conceiving the world, and of acting in it to sustain all life by maintaining the interconnectedness and diversity of nature. ...

[T]he dominant science system emerged as a liberating force not for humanity as a whole (though it legitimised itself in terms of universal betterment of the species), but as a masculine and patriarchal project which necessarily entailed the subjugation of both nature and women. ...

I characterise modern western patriarchy's special epistemological tradition of the 'scientific revolution' as 'reductionist' because it reduced the capacity of humans to know nature both by excluding other knowers and other ways of knowing, and it reduced the capacity of nature to creatively regenerate and renew itself by manipulating it as inert and fragmented matter. ...

Women in sustenance economies, producing and reproducing wealth in partnership with nature, have been experts in their own right of a holistic and ecological knowledge of nature's processes.

(Shiva, 1989, cited from Smith, 1999, pp.325–9)

Eco-feminists like Shiva have argued that the attempt to dominate and control nature is a product of a specifically male way of reasoning that developed in the post-medieval West, a 'science' that was reductionist and based on the

FIGURE 3.8 A woman who lived in trees for six months to prevent the construction of the M65 motorway extension, Stamworth Valley, Lancashire

suppression of women's ways of knowing the natural world. The mechanistic view of the world as governed by abstract laws, with spirit expunged from the material world, is seen by Carolyn Merchant, for example, as a specifically masculine and patriarchal way of knowing (1980; see also Wertheim, 1997). That is to say, these thinkers argue not only that our thinking has been anthropocentric but that it has become **androcentric**. Drawing on these ideas, eco-feminist thinkers have maintained that women's values of nurture and care, as distinct from the 'male' values of dominion and control, provide a more appropriate model of reverence for nature and of ecological care. (These ideas have not gone unchallenged by other liberal and socialist feminists.)

Androcentrism
A view which is dominated by the concerns of men and which marginalizes or obscures the interests of women.

By contrast, other thinkers sympathetic to ecologism seek a middle path between the rejection of the exploitative practices of Western science advocated by Shiva, on the one side, and the confidence expressed in scientific reason by all the modern political ideologies, on the other. As Anthony Giddens has noted:

> Some have said that the very idea of inanimate nature, so significant to the outlook and technology of the modern West, should be rejected today. Thus Rupert Sheldrake has suggested that 'once again it makes sense to think of nature as alive'; we might think of 'the entire cosmos' as 'more like a developing organism than an external machine'. This process he specifically connects with the rebirth of tradition and ritual, as well as with an exploration of religion. 'A number of Westerners, myself included, have rejected the Christian religion and explored instead the religious traditions of the East, particularly Hinduism and Buddhism; others have attempted to revive aspects of pre-Christian paganism and the religion of the goddess'.
>
> (Giddens, 1994, p.78, quoting Sheldrake, 1990, pp.153, 154)

Similarly, John Polkinghorne, a theoretical physicist who later became an Anglican priest, introduces his discussion of the relation between scientific and religious belief as follows:

> From the practice of science to the acknowledgement of moral duty, on to aesthetic delight and religious experience, we live in a world which is the carrier of value at all levels of our meeting with it. Only a metaphysical account which is prepared to acknowledge that this is so can be considered to be at all adequate.
>
> (Polkinghorne, 1998, p.19)

We started by noting how ecologism developed out of biology and physics and we have ended by seeing how eco-feminism challenges anthropocentrism by criticizing androcentric science. Green politics itself remains divided by these questions. There are currents within radical ecology which turn towards 'spiritual' enlightenment as a means of responding to the environmental crisis, while others put their 'faith' in science. Still others, like Polkinghorne, see no necessary conflict between the spiritual and the scientific.

ACTIVITY 3.7

Before reading any further, try to make some entries in the 'Economics', 'Politics' and 'Culture' boxes in the column, 'Green alternatives', in Table 3.1 on page 87.

SUMMARY

- We have explored the radical environmental idea that it is possible to operate on a fundamentally different moral and cultural basis from the conventional notions of self-interest and instrumental reason. This intuition is captured in two central ideas: firstly, that non-human nature constitutes a source of value and interest in its own right; and secondly, that we should seek to overcome our anthropocentric perspectives.

- Ecology as a science and ecologism as a political ideology derive from a combination of a biological understanding of the place of human beings in the natural world and a physical understanding of the ultimate limits of energy and time in our economic activities.

- This new understanding of the natural constraints on human social organization calls into question the notions of efficiency and progress found in conventional economic thinking which modern political ideologies rely upon.

- The meaning of nature has changed from one society to another and from one time to another. At different times and in different places, nature has been evaluated and responded to in varying ways. The meanings of nature and the kinds of action that flow from them are now being contested again within and beyond green thinking.

- One specific candidate for a new (or renewed) valuation of nature is the eco-feminist conception which is critical of the androcentric position alleged to characterize modern science. The compatibility of scientific understandings of nature with those derived from other traditions of thought, including spiritual ones, remains hotly debated.

5 EVALUATING MODERN POLITICAL IDEOLOGIES

ACTIVITY 3.8

Compare the ideas or answers that you have put into the boxes in the second column of Table 3.1 on page 87, 'Responses of modern political ideologies' and those that you have noted in the column, 'Green alternatives'.

- How would you characterize the main differences between the responses of the modern political ideologies and the green alternatives?

- What do you think are the strengths and weaknesses of each?

- How convincing do you find the responses of the modern political ideologies?

- How compelling do you think is the case for a green alternative?

COMMENT

Now look at my attempt to complete the table, shown overleaf in Table 3.2, and compare your answers with mine. Remember that my comments that follow the table are based on how I have filled it in. If your answers are different from mine, then you will probably evaluate the modern political ideologies and the green alternatives somewhat differently as well. This is an inevitable feature of ideological evaluation, since ideologies are not exhausted by their factual content but have important prescriptive and normative components. Deciding between these components involves making choices not only about what we think is happening but also about what we want for the future.

TABLE 3.2   Summary of environmental problems for political ideologies

	Environmental problems of modern political ideologies	Responses of modern political ideologies	The challenge of green thinking	Green alternatives
Economics	Continued world-wide industrialization is not environmentally sustainable The market cannot solve environmental problems	The problem is not one of how <u>much</u> growth but what <u>kind</u> of growth to pursue Many environmental problems can be solved by markets if environmental resources are owned and priced properly	Environmental problems are often unknown and complex Money is not the measure of everything What about the future?	Reorganize society away from material growth towards spiritual development Replace the market with self-sufficiency and direct popular control
Politics	Environmental problems are typically global in their causes and effects, whereas political authority and control is exercised on a national basis	International co-operation is possible on the basis of self-interest among states, especially when knowledge about the problem is available and agreed	If problems are global in scope, then we must move beyond the nation-state and organize politics at a global level as well	Encourage the development of global citizenship and reconstitute political authority at a global level through extending the UN system
Culture	Environmental problems are evidence that we cannot subject nature to our control without creating problems	We are part of nature and therefore we must take an enlightened view of our own interests, which include a healthy environment	Enlightened self-interest is still <u>self</u>-interest (it's human-centred), but what about the interests of the rest of nature?	Respect and protect the interests of the non-human natural world Need for a new spiritualism Need for non-reductionist, non-individualistic forms of thinking

While we must be careful not to lump all the modern political ideologies together (as we saw in Section 3.1, there are some important differences between them) and we must not exaggerate the differences between them and the green alternatives (for example, compare Sections 3.1 and 4.3), some broad differences of emphasis do stand out.

The responses of modern political ideologies are very much based on modifications to a set of basically modern assumptions. If environmental problems are uncertain and complex, then let's have more science. If the market isn't registering environmental consequences, then let's incorporate environmental values into the monetary economy. If national politics can't cope with trans-border issues, then let's organize international co-operation. If narrow self-interest is neglecting the natural environmental basis of our well-being, then let's be more enlightened. In short, let's continue as we are, only more intelligently.

By contrast, green alternatives emphasize a break with or a departure from modernist assumptions. If we don't know what we are doing, then let's reverse the burden of proof for economic and technological development. If growth is a problem, let's encourage self-sufficiency and non-material (spiritual) development. If the national level cannot cope, let's develop a global consciousness and politics. And, perhaps most importantly of all, if our inherited ways of thinking about what we value have led us astray, then let's develop new (or renew old) ways of thinking about our place in nature.

We can link the evaluation of these positions back to our starting idea that political ideologies in some senses form maps. Political ideologies seek to answer certain questions about how society is organized, how it works and how it might be different. In addressing these questions we have suggested that they face a double challenge – they must be intellectually coherent to some extent, otherwise we couldn't believe in them, and they must have some practical adequacy, or else they would serve no useful purpose for us. We have to be able both to read and to use the map. Green thinking claims that the nature of environmental degradation produced by societies governed by modern political ideologies is such that new maps are needed to point us in new directions in our relations with nature. Defenders of the modern political ideologies argue that the old maps are still serviceable, but that they may require some redrawing to deal with the new terrain. The modified modern political ideologies and the green alternatives now compete for our allegiance and both will be tested intellectually and practically in the future. Whether the outcome of this will result in the displacement of the modern political ideologies by the green alternatives, or the successful adaptation of the former to the critiques of the latter, only time and events will tell. In the meantime, as citizens we will have to make some choices, we will individually and collectively have to decide which maps to use. And different maps will take us to different places.

SUMMARY

- There are important differences between the political ideologies of modernity and the newer green thinking. Green thinking itself now competes with the established modern ideologies.

- We can understand modern political ideologies and green thinking as rival maps for the future, and the ongoing debate between these views of the world, as well as their practical achievements, will have profound consequences for our future and that of the environment in which we live.

REFERENCES

Arnold, D. (1996) *The Problem of Nature: Environment*, Oxford, Basil Blackwell.

Cochrane, A. and Pain, K. (2004) 'A globalizing society?' in Held, D. (ed.).

Boulding, K. (1966) 'The economics of the coming Spaceship Earth' in Jarret, H. (ed.) *Environmental Quality in a Growing Economy*, Baltimore; MD, John Hopkins University Press.

Bramwell, A. (1989) *Ecology in the 20th Century*, New Haven, Yale University Press.

Freeden, M. (1996) *Ideologies and Political Theory*, Oxford, Clarendon Press.

Giddens, A. (1994) 'Living in a post-traditional society', in Beck, U., Giddens, A. and Lash, S., *Reflexive Modernization*, Cambridge, Polity.

Hayward, T. (1998) *Political Theory and Ecological Values*, Cambridge, Polity.

Held, D. (ed.) (2004) *A Globalizing World? Culture, Economics, Politics* (2nd edn), London, Routledge/The Open University.

Himmelweit, S. and Simonetti; R. (2004) 'Nature for sale' in Hinchliffe, S. and Woodward, K. (eds).

Hinchliffe, S. (2004) 'Living with risk: the unnatural geography of environmental crises' in Hinchliffe, S. and Woodward, K. (eds).

Hinchliffe, S. and Woodward, K. (eds) (2004) *The Natural and the Social: Uncertainty, Risk, Change* (2nd edn), London, Routledge/The Open University.

Illich, I. (1973) *Energy and Equity*, London, Calder & Boyars.

McGrew, A. (2004) 'Power shift: from national government to global governance' in Held, D. (ed.).

Merchant, C. (1980) *The Death of Nature,* New York, Harper & Row.

O'Neill, J. (1993) *Ecology, Policy and Politics*, London, Routledge.

Polkinghorne, J. (1998) *Belief in God in an Age of Science*, New Haven, Yale University Press.

Porritt, J. (1984) *Seeing Green*, Oxford, Basil Blackwell.

Quinton, A. (1978) *The Politics of Imperfection*, London, Faber and Faber.

Sandler, T. (1997) *Global Challenges*, Cambridge, Cambridge University Press.

Sheldrake, R. (1990) *The Rebirth of Nature*, London, Rider.

Shiva, V. (1989) *Staying Alive*, London, Zed Books.

Smith, M. (ed.) (1999) *Thinking Through the Environment*, London, Routledge.

Soper, K. (1995) *What Is Nature?*, Oxford, Basil Blackwell.

Wertheim, M. (1997) *Pythagoras' Trousers*, London, Fourth Estate.

Williams, R. (1976) *Keywords*, London, Fontana.

World Bank (1992) *World Development Report*, Oxford, Oxford University Press.

FURTHER READING

John Polkinghorne (1996) *Beyond Science*, Cambridge, Cambridge University Press.

A discussion of the nature and place of scientific belief in its wider human context by a former theoretical physicist who later became an Anglican priest.

Tim Hayward (1998) *Political Theory and Ecological Values*, Cambridge, Polity.

A very clear discussion of what it might mean to value the environment for its own sake and how doing so changes our understanding of what is politically right and just.

Anna Bramwell (1989) *Ecology in the 20th Century*, New Haven, Yale University Press.

A history of ecological thought, tracing it from its origins in the late nineteenth century through to its revival in the 1970s, set in the context of wider social and cultural developments.

John O'Neill (1993) *Ecology, Policy and Politics*, London, Routledge.

A wide-ranging discussion of our place in the natural world and of how our economic and political institutions might take account of this.

Changing times, changing knowledge

Kath Woodward, David Goldblatt and Liz McFall

Contents

1 INTRODUCTION – KNOWING THE SOCIAL SCIENCES

The focus of this book so far has been on changing knowledge; knowledge about societies and the knowledge that is produced by the social sciences. This focus on change suggests that the world we live in is being transformed, perhaps at a faster rate than at previous moments in history. There are, of course, continuities, but *how* we know about the changes that are taking place is a fast moving field. There is dispute about the extent of change as well as debate about the benefits and advantages of the changes that may be taking place and this chapter covers different approaches. We consider some of the ways in which change and the growth of knowledge can be seen as beneficial and desirable on the one hand as well as, on the other hand, creating greater anxiety. However, we would like to start by exploring in a bit more detail the claim that knowledge is particularly important in contemporary societies and by offering a discussion of what we mean by the term 'the **knowledge society**'.

Knowledge society
A term used to describe those societies in which knowledge is the motor for social, economic, cultural and political development and change.

This term is used to describe and explain the importance of knowledge in contemporary societies. Knowledge has always been important. However, whereas traditional societies may have venerated seniority, age and established knowledge, more recently priority has been accorded to change and to the new. The knowledge society refers in particular to those societies in which knowledge (which includes ideas, ways of thinking and practices) provides the instigator of change and development within the fields of economic, social, cultural and political life. For example, professional knowledge, innovation and new ideas can be more important than the raw materials from which products are made. Access to information, ideas and new practices constitutes the motor for change, and knowledge carries more weight than other resources. Another aspect of knowledge in contemporary societies is the *speed* of knowledge production and dissemination. It has become possible to transmit knowledge across space, for example globally, very quickly in ways that were inconceivable until very recently. It is the knowledge of new technologies that permit the developments that are taking place in our everyday lives as well as in global organization.

In order to characterize different forms of social relations and to explain change, we need to look at what sorts of knowledge are created in society, and to what use new knowledge is put and who has access to these knowledges. Power, including political and economic power, operates through knowledge systems and those who have the relevant, often specialized knowledge that triggers change are more powerful than those who do not. The argument that we live in a knowledge society puts knowledge systems first in the analysis, rather than seeing access to knowledge as secondary to other aspects of social relations like political or economic structures. Knowledge has a key role to play in explaining power relations and social structures.

Now that we have introduced the idea of the 'knowledge society' and indicated some of its features, Chapter 4 will:

- Explain some of the historical, economic and social background that led to the advent of the knowledge society and how social scientists have characterized these developments.

- Explore some of the outcomes and manifestations of the knowledge society, such as anxiety and the growing awareness of risk and how the plurality of knowledge systems and information sources might democratize society and/or undermine sources of certainty.

1.1   Knowledge and the social sciences

Much of the focus upon knowledge comes from the social sciences and the expansion of academic research into the impact of different systems for the production and transmission of knowledge. The very notion of a 'knowledge society' itself comes from the social sciences. This is why we focus on knowledge in this book; we have picked it up as being a central, substantive concern in the contemporary world and in the social sciences. The social sciences, which are themselves involved in producing knowledge, are also instrumental in effecting change in particular ways. For example, concepts developed within the social sciences to explain social, economic, cultural, political and psychological phenomena have become part of the common currency of everyday communication. Concepts employed to provide a focus upon some of the key concerns at all levels in contemporary life, such as identity, globalization, ideology and the unconscious, shape what could be called 'common sense' understandings of change. Some of the ideas that were once the concern of academic research have become part of everyday life, through media coverage and dissemination on the internet and through other popular cultural forms. The social changes identified in this book, in relation to science and medicine, religion, politics and the environment, have all been subjects of inquiry in the social sciences, as has been demonstrated in the first three chapters. The knowledge produced through this research and study has shaped our understanding of these areas of experience and has often provided us with the concepts through which we make sense of our own experience of change. The social sciences respond to change, but are also implicated in the forms those changes take, whether through the ideas they generate, through the methods of inquiry that they deploy or through the actions that might be implicated in the explanations and theories that they offer. This means looking at *what* we know as social scientists; *how* we know and what we *do* with what we know. The first three chapters of this book have been organized respectively around the questions that are implicated in the last statement.

1   What is knowledge?

2   How do we know things?

3   What do we do about what we know?

1.2   What is knowledge?

To start with our first question, what is knowledge? This was the focus of Chapter 1, which examined the social construction of different kinds of knowledge about medicine and medical science. The key issue is the nature of knowledge; what counts as knowledge? Knowledge includes the ideas, practices, ways of thinking and doing in more or less organized forms that range from sophisticated academic knowledge embodied in highly regarded texts, such as those of the medical scientific establishment, to the common sense, routine practices of our daily lives, such as looking after ourselves and our children. What is this knowledge about and how is it made up? What are the different dimensions of the process of **social construction**? The idea of social construction includes the context within which knowledge is produced and all the different processes that are involved.

Social constructionism, as a particular theoretical approach, also refers to the claim that all knowledge is produced, that there is no 'truth' or 'reality' outside the processes through which knowledge is created. Thus it could be argued that social scientists produce rather than discover or reveal knowledge. An example of this approach is given in Chapter 1 in the work of Michel Foucault.

However, our main concern in this book is with the processes that are involved; *how* is knowledge produced? We are not directly concerned with the epistemological questions about the status of truth or falsity in relation to the social world. In order to investigate the nature of these very different sorts of knowledge we need to look at the relationship between the producers of knowledge and the source of knowledge, that is, what it is about, and to see them as inextricably interconnected in the social construction of knowledge.

What counts as knowledge is changing. For example, the new technologies that permit the transmission of knowledge at high speed across the globe have had enormous impact on people's daily lives as well is in the operation of international companies and in global political relations. New technologies may not only offer new media, such as contemporary versions of the printing press, which indicate new vehicles for the transmission of knowledge, but they may transform power relations and ultimately what counts as knowledge.

New knowledges take a variety of different forms. Another characteristic of contemporary life is the ever increasing plethora of sources of knowledge, the

Social construction
The ways in which knowledge is socially constructed; for example through language, social, political and legal institutions and through the exercise of power.

Social constructionism
A theoretical approach that prioritizes the social processes that are involved in the production of knowledge. Social constructionists claim that the truth or falsity of knowledge depends upon the circumstances and context within which it is produced.

multiple sites at which knowledge is created as well as disseminated. As we know from our daily lives, in which we are inundated with information about the risks we are taking with our health, our bodies, our pensions, our jobs and our relationships. There are myriad sites at which we might seek knowledge about aspects of life that hitherto we might not have known existed. This is apparent in the range of 'experts' upon whom people may call: relationship experts, financial planners, therapists, counsellors, many of whom draw upon the knowledge that is produced within the social sciences in order to establish their own authority. Knowledge produces meanings; social science produces and creates meanings and ways of understanding social relations.

In recent years, the status of expert knowledge has been changing. Old certainties have perhaps been replaced by new orthodoxies, but there has certainly been some movement and some fragmentation. There has been something of a shift from the established expertise of traditional sources of knowledge, for example in health care from traditional medicine, in religion from orthodox sources and in politics from the historically established political parties. New orthodoxies emerge, ranging from the challenge of new forms of spirituality and complementary health practices to new, non-hierarchical political movements. What could be called the 'knowledge revolution' has created an explosion of new sites for the production and transmission of knowledge. This explosion might seem to offer greater equality and democracy in access to knowledge since it has been accompanied by an expansion of popular culture and a breakdown of the barriers between 'high' and 'low' culture as identified by social scientists (Hall, 1997).

It becomes more difficult to identify the 'expert'. In our everyday lives in the West we are confronted with the rise of the celebrity who, just by virtue of being famous, imparts 'expert' knowledge on a whole range of topics, ranging from pregnancy and childcare through sports and fashion to politics and the environment (see Figure 4.1 overleaf). New knowledge becomes important through being present in the public domain, for example through media coverage. A celebrity whose rise to fame has been through one channel, for example sport, becomes an authority on a completely different subject.

There are different ways of viewing these changes. Do they present a more democratic society that permits everyone to speak? It seems more democratic. The closed doors of expertise and established authority might be opened by this move towards more equality, access and a level playing field. However, this knowledge explosion might also create feelings of uncertainty and risk. Some of the developments of new forms of knowledge may be productive and beneficial while others, especially the breakdown of established sources of certainty, may be unsettling and even dangerous. It is these challenges that offer some of the most fruitful ground for the social sciences in exploring questions about the status of different forms of knowledge in a climate of change.

FIGURE 4.1   David Beckham: more expert on fashion than football?

Within the social sciences there has been some movement from a concern with what *is* knowledge to what *counts as* knowledge. However, it is still the case that some knowledge carries more weight than others. All knowledge production is situated; all knowledge is widely enmeshed in the operations of *power.* Power is contentious and disputed, but has to be included in ways in which knowledge is produced within the social sciences. The debates have shifted to accommodate an analysis of power and recognition of its diffuse operations.

1.3   How do we know things?

Chapter 2 shifted the focus from what constitutes knowledge to a concern with how we go about producing knowledge in the social sciences, using the empirical vehicle of religious knowledge and the study of religious practices. The chapter introduced a debate within the social sciences that focuses on the collection of evidence: a debate on the strengths and weaknesses of the positivist and interpretavist approaches and the different uses of quantitative and qualitative methods. These two different research methods are informed by different theoretical emphases, although, as the chapter suggests, social scientists often need to employ both quantitative *and* qualitative research methods in the same study. Religious affiliation and practice, the ways in which religious knowledge is produced and disseminated, offer an interesting and complex area of study. As is argued in the chapter, while numbers attending a place of worship might give some indication of the extent of involvement in religious practice and belief, merely counting the numbers provides only limited information, especially about people's personal investment in religious beliefs and knowledge.

Chapter 2 focused on some of the ways through which social scientists produce knowledge as well as exploring some of the particular ways in which religious knowledge, as an illustration of a specific set of knowledges, is established, reproduced and reconstructed. The chapter explores a particular narrative of social change and considers different ways of finding out about these changes. In this sense it is a chapter about the methods that are used in the social sciences. The social sciences, in conducting studies into change (for example into the experience and construction of religious knowledge and practice), are also involved in influencing some of those changes. In this example that influence is exerted firstly in the public dissemination of findings and secondly through the methods that have been adopted more widely in other areas of social and economic life.

1.4   What do we do about what we know?

In Chapter 3, Simon Bromley concentrates on another area of change and challenge to traditional sources of knowledge: the challenge to political ideologies posed by the problems of large-scale environmental degradation. Changing times that are marked by world-wide problems of damage to the environment demand political responses that seek to address these problems. By looking at the responses of traditional political ideologies and the emergence of newer political groupings, such as the green movement and feminist ecological movements, it is possible to examine the links between knowledge and social change. The green movement is characterized by a commitment to action and the production of new knowledges, for example, about what constitutes nature, the connections between human agency and the social world and that which is defined as natural. Our knowledge about the natural world cannot be unmediated and Chapter 3 looks at some of the particular ways in which this knowledge is produced in the context of economic, material, social and political change. Environmental matters offer powerful examples illustrating the interrelationship between human actions, whether economic, social or political, and environmental change. This discussion highlights the uncertainties that are increasingly created by problems of environmental degradation, experienced at all levels of our lives and impacting upon the relationship between global and national concerns. Uncertainty derives from both change itself and, more pressingly, the need to address the extent and range of some of the problems that have been generated by damage to the environment. Knowledge about the scale of these problems may itself be one of the causes of insecurity and uncertainty that some social scientists claim beset the contemporary world.

1.5 Summary

Each of these chapters has focused upon a different set of knowledges and the relationship between each example of knowledge and the social sciences. What has been the role of the social sciences in each of these examples? Each of our investigations into changing times has involved looking both at the processes that show how knowledge is socially constructed and at the processes that are involved in the production of knowledge. As was argued right at the start of this book, our approach involves not just what we think about knowledge but what we do with it. Knowledge includes ideas and practices. As suggested in Chapter 1, there are many different ways of understanding the world and many different ways of producing knowledge about it; ranging from common sense and personal knowledge to expert knowledge and knowledge that is systematically organized and carries authority, including the knowledge that is produced through research in the social sciences. In Chapter 1 we used some explanations from the social sciences to look at different arguments about the status of knowledge and how we might be able to establish some kind of validity. Is the only evidence that counts that which disproves our claims, as the philosopher Karl Popper, whose work was cited in Chapter 1, argues? Whose knowledge carries the most status and authority and how does this authority become challenged and replaced by new ideas and practices? Evelyn Fox-Keller (also cited in Chapter 1) suggested that it is necessary to locate the source of power in order to challenge it and make changes, citing the example of men's power that has been challenged by feminist critiques. Chapter 2 used the example of religious knowledge to explore directly some of the methods that are adopted by social scientists to produce evidence to support or refute the claims that they make. The methods used and developed within the social sciences have wide application for example in market research and attitude and opinion surveys. Chapter 3 shifted the emphasis onto political ideologies and the action that is also involved in the production of knowledge, as an example of knowledge as doing as well as thinking. In this chapter ideologies were deployed to illustrate the links between social change and the social sciences. Political ideologies describe, explain and suggest ways of changing the world. As Karl Marx and Friedrich Engels noted at the end of the *German Ideology*, 'the philosophers have only interpreted the world, in various ways: the point is to change it' (Marx and Engels, 1998, p.170). Without committing to any particular course of political action, as Marx and Engels did, we have argued that understanding and interpreting the world is only useful if that knowledge gives us some idea of what we should do about it. Chapter 3 offers different, competing arguments about both explanation and suggested action, but focuses on the links between knowledge in the social sciences and change in the world in which we live. How can knowledge lead to change?

Chapter 4 focuses on these key questions:

- How is knowledge related to social change?
- What is the impact of the development of knowledge in contemporary society?
- Does the 'knowledge society' create more equality and democracy or greater anxiety and uncertainty?

We have looked at changes in medical and religious knowledge and political knowledge in relation to the environment. What other changes have social scientists identified as being particularly important?

2   SOCIAL CHANGE

● ●

Much of contemporary social science has addressed its efforts to the ways in which society is changing. This section explores one approach to the advent of the knowledge society as an example of such change. Section 3 takes another approach, focusing on economic and social change and the significant shifts in the ways in which goods and services are produced and consumed and, consequently, in the relationship between production and consumption that have taken place. Section 4 looks at a different approach to social change and in particular to the knowledge revolution and considers the growth of anxiety and the risk society.

Social and economic changes have taken different forms. Many of the jobs that were available to the last generation have disappeared and have been replaced by new jobs that require completely different skills; often those involving IT and sophisticated computer literacy. The loss of certain jobs, for example in coal mining and heavy manufacturing industries, has been most marked in particular communities, but this is part of a general trend; the move from manufacturing jobs to those in the service sector. The processes, skills and knowledge required to perform in paid employment have seen significant shifts over the last fifty years, with some of these changes being most apparent in recent years, especially in the case of computerized technologies and communication systems. The consumption of goods and services has become another area where expert advice is available to inform the choices made by consumers.

ACTIVITY 4.1

Think about your own life. Can you think of areas of your life where knowledge demands might have changed or become more intense and diverse? What skills are required in the work you do compared with your parents' generation? These changes can apply to paid and unpaid work, including work in the home such as the work of being a parent and caring for children or elderly, sick or disabled relatives or friends. What sources of knowledge do you turn to for advice and guidance?

COMMENT

Parents are bombarded with a massive range of advice from different sources and are required to make decisions based on the choices that are now available about how best to bring up children. Childcare and other aspects of life in what might have been deemed areas of private and personal, rather than public concern, have increasingly become the target of diverse sets of knowledge. All of these activities, from looking after one's self to looking after children and the domestic environment, have become work that requires some expert knowledge in order to make informed decisions. There is a whole set of new discourses through which knowledge is produced about all aspects of life. Even our personal relationships have become 'work' with a massive range of advice on effective management of relationships, counselling and therapy available within popular culture as well as from 'official' sources. Paid work and the knowledge and skills required have been completely transformed for many people; shopping now demands a high level of expertise!

Consumption of goods and services is a key area for the creation of new 'expert' knowledge. There is a vast amount of information available about products and services and a whole industry is dedicated to providing consumers with advice on making informed choices. Consumers might appear to be not only very knowledgeable but also to exercise power over which goods and services are produced. Everyday life in the affluent countries of Europe, North America and the Pacific Rim, is saturated with an extraordinary quantity and array of goods produced for sale. The desire for more and more things is the very motor of affluent societies with one estimate placing 90 per cent of the US workforce in the business of producing consumer goods and services (Rosenblatt, 1999). These goods and services are not desired simply for what they can **do**, their instrumental or functional nature, but for what they **mean**, their symbolic or communicative features. In contemporary, western society it seems it is not what we do, or where we live that defines our identities but what we buy.

Knowledge about these changes is incredibly widespread. We all have first-hand experience of consumption and may well have our own ideas about what makes this experience different from thirty or forty years ago. The media provide a steady stream of information with regular features exploring both the practicalities of what and how to consume and the politics and ecology of global consumption, with companies clamouring for the distinction of 'consumer orientation'. In academia books on consumer culture are legion across all the disciplines of the humanities and social sciences. Even the public services organizations, from government departments to museums and hospitals, relate to the outside world as 'consumers' or customers rather than taxpayers, patrons or patients. What all these popular, commercial and academic ideas have in common is a generalized sense that what is happening applies across society as a whole and is historically unprecedented.

These changes involve new sets of knowledge, both in relation to how things are made and how services are provided, and in relation to how knowledge is produced and transmitted. What is distinctive about the ways in which some of these changes have been characterized is the emphasis that is given to knowledge in the economic changes that, many have claimed, swept through western societies in the latter part of the twentieth century.

2.1 Post-industrial society

One of the earliest and most influential accounts of these changes has developed out of the writings of the US commentator, Daniel Bell. In his book, *The Coming of Post-Industrial Society* (Bell, 1973), he highlighted the changes that were taking place, in particular, in the USA. Like many others Bell had noticed that the balance of employment between agricultural, extractive and manufacturing sectors of the economy and service sectors had been steadily shifting in favour of the service sector, so that by the late 1960s the US economy was becoming dominated by service employment and manufacturing was shrinking. Given that the major sociological accounts of modern societies had placed the industrial and manufacturing sector and the production process at the heart of their claims, it became clear that a new theoretical framework was required for describing and explaining contemporary societies and exploring their trajectory for change.

Bell's claims about industrial society, which characterized the USA, the UK and other western societies for most of the twentieth century, focused on production and especially the manufacturing sector as the source of male employment, output and dynamism. As a consequence these economies were dominated by the large-scale manufacturing production lines that successful and profitable manufacturing required. Moreover, they were organized along strict hierarchies in which power and authority were firmly at the top.

As a consequence, he argued, the social structure of industrial societies was very close to the model proposed by Marx in the nineteenth century: a small group of capitalists (owners of capital) and managers (employed to run the enterprises for the owners to create profit), exploiting and policing a large, often oppositional manual working class (see **Mackintosh and Mooney, 2004**). These two classes, the owners of capital and the means of production and those who had only their labour to sell were locked into a perpetual class struggle, economically and politically, over the distribution of profits. This situation, Marx argued could not be resolved within the capitalist mode of production, which relied on private ownership of capital. A more equal distribution could only be achieved by the overthrow of this economic system and common ownership of the means of production. Marx predicted a greater polarization of the two classes (the bourgeoisie or capitalist class, and the proletariat or working class) and the inevitably increased exploitation of the working class. However, he acknowledged that capitalism was subject to booms, when there might be short-term gains for the proletariat, along with slumps, which would increase their distress.

The manufacturing sector had emerged in the late nineteenth century at the expense of the rural agricultural sector. Technological and managerial innovations in that era had made agriculture more productive so that more could be produced with less labour. That surplus labour moved from the country to the city where new jobs in manufacturing were emerging and new markets for manufactured goods were developing. The same processes of increasing productivity through technological innovation, large capital investment, and the development of new needs and wants among the public would, according to Bell, lead to the shrinking of the manufacturing sector and the expansion of the service sector.

The chain of causation would run like this: investment in automation and robotics and the adoption of new rationalized management techniques would allow manufacturing firms to produce more and more goods with fewer and fewer employees. The massive increase in wealth this would generate would in turn stimulate the creation of new needs and wants among the newly enriched consuming public. The demand for social services, higher education and advanced health care could be expected to rise, as would the demand for more leisure activities: shopping, tourism and restaurants. Happily, the workers steadily released from the manufacturing sector would be able to take up jobs in the new service sector. Moreover, because, according to Bell, services are dependent upon personal contact and emotional skills, their capacity for automation is very limited. Services are unlikely to be shrunk in the same way that manufacturing was. So, an upward spiral of increasing industrial wealth turning into new service needs and new service employment would be created.

The post-industrial society would be characterized by more than a shift in sectoral employment. Bell came to argue that it would be a society in which the basis of wealth and power would shift and, in turn, new patterns of social stratification, politics and culture would emerge. At the core of the post-industrial society would be theoretical knowledge and those who generated, manipulated and used it. While Bell was always a little coy about precisely what constituted theoretical knowledge, he was predominantly referring to codified, systematic, abstract systems of knowledge: conventional medical science, applied psychiatry, the social sciences and other knowledge embedded in the institutions that legitimize it. This was not common sense, every day knowledge. These forms of knowledge could be cumulatively developed and systematically applied to a wide range of economic and social processes as opposed to tacit, implicit and practical knowledge whose capacity for transfer was limited and whose application was dependent on a specific context. For example management skills could be applied across a range of different contexts. The processes of automation, as well as the production of advanced services (such as education and medicine) were all dependent on theoretical knowledge. The creators and guardians of theoretical knowledge, who Bell referred to as *professionals*, would become the dominant social class in post-industrial societies. Simultaneously, with the decline of employment in the manufacturing sector, the manual working class would shrink to be replaced by a labour force of predominantly white-collar workers. While classical forms of class struggle, between capital and labour would not entirely disappear, they would cease to be the central axis around which the politics of advanced societies would revolve. Professionals would be guided and driven by motivations other than profit and loss. All professionals would seek to use rational planning as a mode of social organization rather than rely on the anarchy of the market. White-collar workers, no longer subject to the exploitative regimes of harsh industrial labour and low wages, would cease to perceive all their political and economic interests in class terms. What would separate these groups would be culture rather than economics, for the elite and the masses would be divided by their access to theoretical knowledge. Bell suggested that the gulf might be so wide that people might not be able to share a common culture (Bell, 1976); if they ever had. Bell's predictions countered our claim at the start of this chapter that knowledge production and transmission is becoming more democratic and equal.

2.1.1   The knowledge economy

At the start of the twenty-first century we might like to revisit Bell's arguments, to consider the extent of the knowledge revolution that he anticipated and to address other developments that he could not have included. It is clear that the relative weight, in employment terms, of manufacturing and services has decisively shifted in favour of the latter. We have seen the virtual demise of the coal industry in the UK and the decline of steel production and of heavy manufacturing industries such as car production. However, in at least two important ways the core assumptions of his model of the knowledge society have been superseded. Firstly, the key technologies of change are no longer automation processes alone, they have been joined by the enormous range of communication and information technologies that were in their infancy in the early 1970s: advanced telecommunications, computers and the internet. Secondly, it has been argued that the theoretical knowledges that Bell saw as central to social change have had their major impact, not in the realm of public and private service provision, but right at the heart of the manufacturing economy. The development of new material sciences such as biotechnology and telecommunications have led to both a shift in the organization of production and a transformation of what is produced and of how goods are produced. As a consequence, in the late 1990s, new models of a post-industrial knowledge society have emerged that embrace these profound social changes. In this extract Charles Leadbeater illustrates some of the ways in which these changes are experienced in our everyday lives:

> The personal computer I am using to write this essay has about the same amount of gold, silicon, copper and other metals as the computer I used five years ago. Both machines weigh and look much the same. But today's machine is twenty times more powerful than the older machine. The difference is entirely to do with the way in which the physical components have been rearranged. That difference comes from human intelligence, rearranging the available physical materials to make them more productive. That is the story of modern economic growth. Improvements in productivity and wealth largely come from human ingenuity: our finding cleverer ways to combine the basic physical components available to us on or just below the earth's crust.
>
> Take two more examples: the humble drinks can and a blade of wheat. Twenty or 30 years ago, drinks cans were so heavy it took an act of strength to crush them. These days drinks cans are made of ultra-thin, ultra-light material. The can's shape is maintained in large part by the liquid inside it. Today's drink can is 80 per cent lighter than twenty years ago because science has allowed it to be made of lighter materials. The modern can is 80 per cent know-how, 20 per cent materials. Knowledge has replaced metal. Similarly, the average blade of wheat is 80 per cent more productive than wheat in the 1930s because scientists and breeders have learned how to grow more productive, robust strains. The main grain of wheat is 80 per cent know-how.
>
> (Leadbeater, 1998, pp.11–12)

At the core of his argument is the idea that the things that are used to produce goods and services are changing from what we can see and touch to factors that are intangible. While the manufacturing giants of the mid-twentieth century prospered by combining huge quantities of raw materials, fixed plant (factories and machines) and semi-skilled labour, the successful economies and corporations of the future will prosper on an asset base of scientific knowledge, highly skilled staff and, of equal importance, marketing knowledge.

Even in those areas of production that one might not immediately think of as involving the highest specialist technologies, like the clothing industry, there have been enormous technological innovations in recent years. For example in the UK the large-scale companies, such as Marks & Spencer, Next and Benetton, have adopted the strategy of sub-contracting to small, low technology companies by using new computer-aided design and computer-controlled cutting. Such technologies have made it easier to store designs, make modifications and shift between different designs for short production runs. They have also allowed production decisions to wait until the latest sales information became available. This method of production (leaving it to the last minute) was closely linked to other new technologies such as EPOS (Electronic Point Of Sale) when details of sales are electronically recorded at the till. EPOS allows information about sales and stock levels to be fed directly back into production and product runs can be adjusted accordingly. The fashion chain Zara (see Figure 4.2) specializes in selling designer clothes at high street prices, by controlling manufacturing more closely than its competitors (and *not* by advertising).

FIGURE 4.2   Zara – fast fashion on the high street

Other technological developments have improved the speed and efficiency of communication networks. Prior to the communications revolution, communications technologies were relatively simple and relatively expensive. Although telephone and television became more widely available each presented significant limits to the amount of information that could be transmitted and had heavy cost implications. Television was still a one-way street rather than being interactive. More recently, the processing power and cost of computers has tumbled as silicon chips have become much cheaper and more powerful. The advent of the fibre optic cable, reliable satellite transmission and the digitalization of telephony have made telecommunications infinitely cheaper, more accessible and more adaptable. It has become more cost effective for UK companies to locate their customer response centres far away from the UK and far from the locality of the customer in order to rationalize costs and time-scales. For example banks no longer offer a local voice, whether of the bank manager or any other person located at the nearest branch, but prefer to employ computerized technologies with which far distant operatives respond to customers' calls and access their banking details. Call centre operatives in India are trained in the 'British way of life' in order to deal with enquiries from customers who telephone what they may think is the number of the local branch of their bank.

Francis Cairncross (1997) argues that the new communications technologies have been key to the globalization of finance. Firstly, foreign exchange, government bonds, private stocks and shares and investments of all kinds can now be traded on a global basis around the clock, with transactions crossing national borders and evading national regulations with impunity. Finance and capital have become increasingly intangible assets too. Secondly, the location and size of corporations are no longer significant competitive advantages. Most companies do not need to be physically near sources of raw materials, their customers or even staff if all communication is electronic. The relative cheapness of these technologies combined with global access to capital means that small companies can start up easily and be as competitive as large companies. Both of these forces raise the degree of competition in product markets while information technologies allow consumers to search quickly, and at almost minimal cost, for the best bargains. So once again branding is important to corporate survival and the discovery of new market niches and new consumers through information processing is increasing in importance. However, it is not all one sided; although consumers can access information quickly and cheaply and exercise some agency in selecting relevant information about products and services, they are also bombarded with information by companies that are ever anxious to seek out new markets and consumers.

To cite the example of advertising, where television and other media have been used extensively to promote products and to shape consumption, it is most recently that the complete range of complex technologies have been fully deployed. These technologies permit a bewildering and unprecedented array of techniques to inform, persuade, entertain and seduce consumers. Contemporary advertising employs moving and fixed images, sound, music and text across a range of technologically differentiated media, analogue and digital cable and satellite television, free-to-air terrestrial television, electronic bill boards, video streaming, cinema and web casts. These new technologies take on an all-embracing, all-pervasive cultural and social role. Enabled and enhanced by technology, advertising is widely understood as one of the primary social developments within the knowledge society. How can we resist? Are these forms of knowledge that manipulate rather than inform? How far does this explosion of knowledge make us all 'experts'? These questions are addressed in Sections 3 and 4 below. There are other changes that have contributed to the shifts that we have identified in the moves from an emphasis on consumption rather than production and the increasing primacy of knowledge in relation to social change, that we want to explore further first.

SUMMARY

- Many of the social and economic changes in the late twentieth century have involved the production and transmission of knowledge.

- The material aspects of production have changed to give priority to new forms of knowledge in the processes of production.

- New technologies have permitted a speedier transmission of knowledge that has had very significant effects upon social relations and spatial organization, transcending the boundaries of nation states and permitting very fast access to knowledge and a vastly accelerated speed of transmission. This may not change the substance of what is transmitted but it still has material implications on production, consumption, social relations and employment.

3 FROM PRODUCTION TO CONSUMPTION

Section 2 focused on the knowledge explosion that characterized what we have called the 'knowledge society'. This section introduces another approach to social and economic change, which is also implicated in the growth of knowledge systems, by concentrating on the shift in emphasis from production to consumption. Section 3 also looks at the 'consumer society', as an example of another area where there has been a huge expansion of knowledge.

Not only have economic changes and changes in production been characterized by new technologies (especially computerized technologies) but there have been transformations in the relationship between production and consumption. In their attempt to explain this phenomenon, many social scientists have moved away from the Marxist emphasis on the relations of *production* as the key determinants of social relations, and have focused more upon *consumption* as a key stage in economic processes. These shifts have been characterized in different ways. One approach has been to mark the move from Fordist methods of production to those that have been described as post-Fordist. In order to consider the implications of this in more detail we need to look at what was involved in Fordist economic systems.

3.1 Fordism

The period immediately following the Second World War has been characterized by social scientists as Fordist. This term has been used to describe an economic system the practical origins and inspiration of which can in part be traced back to the programme of corporate organization and politics pursued by Henry Ford in the first few decades of the twentieth century, but which was only diffused and entrenched across entire economies (rather than in a single car company) after 1945. This was a period characterized by mass production. Ford's innovations were actually less revolutionary than many have claimed, and his re-organization of work and production had some parallels in other parts of the US economy. Nonetheless his impact was very significant. Car production before Ford had been characterized by high cost, luxury cars on very short production runs. Labour was highly skilled, highly demarcated and retained a considerable degree of autonomy from management over working practices. Above all, workers came to the motor car in the factory rather than the other way round. In a series of factories built in the first three decades of the twentieth century, Ford changed all of this. His factories produced low-cost, high-volume cars for a mass market (see Figure 4.3). The cars were brought to semi-skilled workers on production lines who performed a singular repetitive task before the car moved on. Management hierarchies were strict, direct and very tightly policed. As a consequence Ford was able to manufacture huge numbers of cars at low cost. But, and it is a big 'but', he also argued that workers needed to earn enough money and have enough free time to purchase and enjoy these cars themselves in sufficient numbers so that his massive investment in plant and machinery could be turned into profit. Mass production required mass consumption.

FIGURE 4.3   Mass car production at Ford's Trafford Park plant in Manchester (1914)

3.2 Post-Fordism

Although there are considerable differences between the work of Daniel Bell and more recent accounts of the knowledge society, there are also some similarities. One of the assumptions of all such work is that the economy in question is a capitalist economy; an economy in which the ownership of property and capital is overwhelmingly private and in which there are competitive markets for capital, goods and labour. The accounts of social scientists are written within the context of changes within capitalism however and respond to some of these changes within capitalist production and consumption. Post-Fordist writing focuses on the move from mass production to flexible specialization with products becoming more customized and individualized. The deregulation of financial markets opened up new modes and new relations of production. These shifts heralded the move to the 'consumer society'.

Post-Fordist theory addresses the importance of the new economic forms of organization that have supplanted the systems of mass production commonly associated with Henry Ford's car company and 'Fordism'. In a post-Fordist economy new technologies facilitate shorter, more varied production runs.

The huge corporations of Fordism gave way to more flexible organization, with a diversified labour force and many activities being out-sourced to small companies. Post-Fordist flexible specialization caters well to the consumer society's stress on the variety of products used as lifestyle accessories, which in turn has allowed for cultural as well as economic change.

Changes in economic systems and production and consumption processes have included the 'turn to culture' that has characterized much of the thinking in the social sciences in the latter part of the twentieth century. The **'cultural turn'** in economics addresses both the increased production of cultural goods (**Mackay, 2004**) and the centrality of culture in the production process, for example through life-style marketing and the focus on the promotion of goods that reproduce and reflect aspirational life styles (du Gay, 1997). This is encapsulated in Figure 4.4 in the play on Descartes' 'Cogito ergo sum' by the artist Barbara Kruger. This involves a different emphasis from that of writers on the 'knowledge society', such as Daniel Bell.

Cultural turn
A move within the social sciences towards the study of the production and consumption of cultural goods and a focus upon the centrality of culture in mediating social relations.

Changing conditions, according to Scott Lash and John Urry (1994) have guided the transition from the Fordist era to the culture industries of the post-Fordist era, through the use of advertising. Zygmunt Bauman identifies the *kind* of consumption as what sets consumer society apart.

> The distinctive mark of the consumer society and its consumerist culture is not, however, consumption as such; not even the elevated and fast rising volume of consumption. What sets the members of the consumer society apart from their ancestors is the emancipation of consumption from its past instrumentality that used to draw its limits – the demise of 'norms' and the new plasticity of 'needs', setting consumption free from functional bonds and absolving it from the need to justify itself by reference to anything but its own pleasurability.
>
> (Bauman, 2001, pp.12–13).

We go shopping because we want to, not because we need to!

3.3 Post-modernism

Post-modernism is identified here as developing out of post-Fordist approaches which focus on consumption and economic systems. As suggested by Zygmunt Bauman in the quotation above contemporary consumer society is distinguished by the meanings that are attached to consumption, rather than its utility. These meanings are produced and represented through symbolic systems, notably through the advertisement of goods and services, as well as through the material culture of those products. Contemporary consumer culture is about desires and wish fulfilment. As Jean Baudrillard has argued, identities in consumer culture are multiple and fragmented and concerned with fantasy and desire (1988). For Baudrillard what marks the contemporary era is cultural:

What is sociologically significant for us, and what marks our era under the sign of consumption, is precisely the generalized re-organization of this primary level in a system of signs which appears to be ... the specific mode of our era.

(Baudrillard, 1988, p.47)

What Baudrillard is getting at is the dominance of a system of needs that is actually produced by the system of production. We 'need' what we can buy. This system is based upon the desire not for material goods as such but for difference and *meaning*. This need for meaning was once met through social ties and networks but these social systems are being progressively overtaken by cultural systems like the media and advertising. Other post-modernist theorizing has linked post-Fordism and post-modernism to the economic changes in production and to the commodification of culture, but Baudrillard stresses the importance of symbolic systems and of *signs*.

The 'signs' to which Baudrillard refers are the meanings associated with the commodities we purchase. By buying the product we buy into the culture and construct our own identities through the association, giving some status to the artist Barbara Kruger's ironic statement: 'I shop therefore I am' (Figure 4.4).

Such post-modernist claims would seem to suggest that the symbol is everything and transcends material factors.

FIGURE 4.4   Shopping for an identity

3.4   We're all experts now?

Does the move from production to consumption in society and the centrality accorded by social scientists to the role of consumption mean that there has been a shift in the distribution of power? Does our access to so many different sources of knowledge mean that we now live in a more democratic society than in years gone by, when society was driven by the motor of production and there was limited access to knowledge for most people?

Today it is relatively easy for shoppers to extend their economic purchasing decisions into political acts or moral statements. Across Western Europe and America, we as consumers can buy specialist magazines and join various movements which seek to inform the consumer about different brands of a type of product. As empowered, information-laden consumers they can try to behave independently of marketing and sales techniques, judging for themselves the quality of a commodity, the fairness of its price, its fitness for the purpose for which it was sold, its safety of use and even the quality of its design aesthetics.

(Daunton and Hilton, 2001, p.1)

Some of the changes that we have considered in this chapter could be read as an indication of a growing transfer of authority from producers to consumers. The 'sovereign' consumer is shorthand in business and marketing circles for an approach to production that claims to put the consumer first by producing what consumers want, rather than selling what producers make. This is different from the argument that consumption has replaced production as the key determinant of social divisions and differentiation, but it retains a focus upon consumption rather than production. The consumer sovereignty argument attributes greater agency to the consumer. Consumer sovereignty is associated with liberal free market thinking. Consumption theories do not necessarily accord agency to the consumer per se but focus on the process of consumption, including the creation of desire. Developments like flexible specialization were informed by the need to make production more sensitive to changes in consumer demand. Innovations in marketing technologies and techniques can also be interpreted as efforts to learn about consumer attitudes and preferences and communicate more effectively with them. Similarly the increased marketization of public services may seem to shift the authority for making judgements about services like education and healthcare away from traditional experts and onto consumers. Consumer authority may thus be a reflection of a broader decline in trust in traditional sources of knowledge and expertise. The increased availability of information about consumption, through the internet, specialist publications such as *Which?*, television and radio programmes and magazines all point to an explosion of knowledge in this field.

3.5   Knowledge of resistance?

However, does more knowledge mean more power? The expansion of knowledge involved could be seen as more an incitement to purchase than a knowledge exchange that creates more genuine choice. More knowledge about products may mean we buy more products, rather than distinguish meaningfully between them.

The shift from production to consumption as part of the explanatory framework of some social science thinking can be criticized for over-emphasizing the degree of choice and freedom that the consumer may exercise and underplaying the damaging outcomes of mass production and the consumer society. For example, the anti-capitalist movement stresses the inequalities of wealth, the conspicuous spending and the externalities, the unintended consequences of the free market (**Himmelweit and Simonetti, 2004**). Academic commentaries share with popular approaches an emphasis on the consumer society as a unique and distinctive phenomenon.

> Since 1950, the industrialized world has been on an unprecedented consumption binge, consuming more goods and services than the combined total of all humans who ever walked on the planet before.
>
> (Taylor and Tilford, 2000, p.463)

This massive boom in consumption has generated resistance, not only through the anti-capitalist movement's campaigns such as the 'Battle of Seattle'. Such campaigns are also fought on the internet through organizations such as Adbusters (see Figure 4.5). Adbusters is part of a movement known as 'culture jamming' that draws on a combination of situationist, surrealist and anarchist principles to counter the logic of the consumerist society. One of their strategies is to 'turn things round' in a 'subvertisement'. Spoof advertisements aim to re-route the spectacular images of advertising to reverse their meanings and thus reclaim control and make consumption 'uncool' (Lasn, 2000, p.424).

FIGURE 4.5   Adbusters and the culture jammers' network

- Economic changes have led to a transformation in the process of production, through Fordism to post-Fordism.
- The knowledge revolution has contributed to these changes.
- There has been a shift in emphasis from production to consumption as a key factor shaping and explaining social relations.
- Post-modernism has highlighted the centrality of culture, both in cultures of production and in the production of culture.

4 TOO MUCH KNOWLEDGE? THE RISK SOCIETY

Our final approach to the knowledge revolution adopts a very different position, focusing upon the 'risk society' and the anxieties that might be associated with the growth of knowledge systems.

Despite the enormous differences in approach of the advocates of the knowledge society, post-modernism and theories of the consumer society they tend to agree that the key shifts that shape modern societies derive from the economy, although post-modernism considers culture and representation as particularly significant to the processes involved. The impact of economic change can be read as more or less influential, as Section 3.5 showed. The unregulated operation of capitalist free markets, promoting wide ranging choice in goods and services, can also have a disastrous impact upon the environment. The German sociologist, Ulrich Beck, has attempted to theorize the transformation of industrial and post-industrial societies and the knowledge revolution in a different fashion (Beck, 1991, 1995). He argues that the key form of knowledge and perception that is instigating social change is neither the communications revolution nor the shift from regulated, planned structures of production but the knowledge, constantly made available to us, that we face the possibility of global catastrophe. Everyone in the western world, indeed globally, has some perception that a nuclear war, accident or irreversible global environmental damage is a real possibility. Beck argues that the social sciences 'have not asked what the threat of self-annihilation means to society, yet there would seem to be general agreement that this is what characterizes and distinguishes the later half of the twentieth century' (Beck, 1995, p.125).

Of course, dangers and hazards have always threatened human societies, much more so in the past than at present, for example the threat of death from disease; infant mortality rates in western countries are very low. What makes them a risk is that they are dangers that are *known*, whose occurrence can be predicted and whose likelihood can be calculated. To be in danger is one thing. To *know* that one is in danger is another. This knowledge also comes at an historical moment when there is high expectation that problems can be solved and danger averted. In pre-industrial society risk took the form of natural hazards, such as earthquakes, drought and plagues. They were effectively unavoidable. Their origins were assigned to external or supernatural forces. With the emergence of industrial societies the social origins, social understanding and social response to risk changed. Risks and accidents become more dependent on the actions of individuals and social groups. The disaster of Chernobyl could be traced to human activity rather than an act of God or a 'natural event (**Himmelweit and Simonetti, 2004, p.80**). Industrial societies developed institutions for dealing with dangers that are not simply the result of natural forces. Beck suggests that the welfare states characteristic of this era should be understood as 'safety states'. The legitimacy of states comes to rest on their capacity to deliver their citizens from both economic risks, like exclusion from the labour market, and environmental risks. These principles have been even more apparent in recent years following the events of 9/11 in 2001 when it appeared that the most powerful of all states, the USA, had been attacked at its heart and needed to demonstrate that the state could ensure the safety of its people. However global terrorism might also pose a threat against which no insurance or safety measures could protect the people of any nation state.

Beck argues that politics have been transformed by the risk society. Industrial politics have changed and traditional political ideologies have been unable to cope with threats that cross traditional state boundaries and defy established forms of regulation (see Chapter 3 this volume). These risks are different in three ways.

- Firstly, neither spatial nor social limitations apply to contemporary hazards. Consider the pollution produced by the nineteenth- or twentieth-century steel mill. The emissions and wastes produced had significant effects on the people who worked at the mill and lived within the local community. However, these did not threaten entire peoples, societies or the planet as a whole. New forms of pollution emerged in the late twentieth century. Beck argues that the toxicity of contemporary environmental risks and their reach into the ecosystem is deeper and more disruptive than the pollutions created in the industrial era. Many of the impacts of these toxins are irreversible and cumulative in their effects.

- Secondly, alongside these everyday toxins, Beck argues that there exist risks that are genuinely catastrophic, for example large-scale nuclear accidents, genetic manipulation of the planet's flora and fauna, global shifts in weather patterns that pose the possibility of global annihilation and total social disruption.

- Thirdly, the point of impact of contemporary environmental risks is not tied to their place of origin. Their transmission and movement are often invisible, which means that they may only be perceived as threats through processes of scientific investigation.

The politics of the risk society is a politics of knowledge, expertise and counter expertise. Beck argues that a politics of knowledge is needed to replace class-based politics. The sharpest difference in this global scenario is not between capital and labour but between those sectors of capital that benefit from the generation of risks, for example the nuclear industry, and those who suffer from the risks of pollution, such as the fishing industry. The role of those who produce and disseminate knowledge increases in importance in such a climate. The social invisibility of contemporary risks means that people are ever more dependent on 'experts' to reveal the extent of those apparently invisible risks. There is conflict, not only over the regulation and control of risks but of the meanings that are attached to the perception of risk. Increasingly politics depends upon the contributions of experts in specialist fields. In spite of this dependence on experts, pledges of certainty become ever more untenable. As Beck puts it:

> With the emergence of the hazards for which they assume (but deny) responsibility, the institutions enter an unwinnable race against the safety claims that have been extorted from them. On the one hand, they end up under the perpetual compulsion to render still safer that which is already as safe as it can be, on the other, people's expectations are thus raised, ultimately intensifying awareness to a point where even the merest suspicion of an accident makes the facades of safety crumble.
>
> (Beck, 1995, p.80)

So, the emergence of new kinds of environmental risks and new knowledge about environmental dangers requires new coping strategies and a new politics based on knowledge. Those forms of risk management that relied upon expert knowledge, that offered claims of certainty and safety, begin to crumble. The risk society has emerged, but it is not a stable society. Indeed it is rife with new forms of conflict, insecurity and disagreement in the realms of knowledge about risks and safety.

SUMMARY

- One of the significant changes in recent years has been the scale of environmental threats.

- Ulrich Beck characterizes contemporary societies as 'risk societies' because of our knowledge of these threats.

- Beck argues that politics have been transformed by the advent of the risk society.

5 WEIGHING UP THE ARGUMENTS

Is there greater democracy? Does the production of knowledge from many different sites and in such easily accessible forms lead to greater equality between members of a society and to the possibility of a more productive society? Or does the proliferation of different sets of knowledge create greater uncertainty and insecurity? In this chapter we have looked at three different approaches to these questions. Firstly, we have considered the view that a range of developments have led to what has been called the 'knowledge society', and cultures in which not only has the dissemination of knowledge become significantly faster and more widespread than at any time in human history, but knowledge is produced and understood in a huge range of different places. Secondly, we have considered the shift from an explanation of social relations based on production to those based on the 'consumer society', where life style and patterns of consumption have become paramount. Thirdly, we have looked briefly at the notion of the 'risk society' and the thesis that knowledge may also increase people's anxiety through the perception of risk. The more we know, the more aware we are of the risks and dangers that beset us in the contemporary world.

ACTIVITY 4.2

Taking each of these three approaches, how would you weigh up their responses to the question: "With the current proliferation of sources of knowledge and the speed of communication is there greater democracy?"

COMMENT _____

The knowledge society thesis parallels the move from production to consumption in its emphasis on new technologies and changing production processes which prioritize knowledge and access to knowledge. However, whereas for Bell this access to knowledge may increase the power of professionals and those who have access to specialist knowledge at the expense of those who do not, for other social scientists the outcome is of greater democracy, for example in the challenge and resistance to dominant ideologies as illustrated in Section 3.5. Some post-modernist approaches see the knowledge revolution as more positive and democratic whereas risk society theories focus upon the anxieties that are created through the plethora of information that people receive about possible dangers, especially in relation to environmental degradation and inner and outer nature. The knowledge revolution has created a heightened awareness of risk, and economic changes have led to a transformation of politics where traditional political systems and strategies have proved incapable of dealing with contemporary risks and dangers.

6 CONCLUSION

● ●

In this chapter we have looked at particular examples of social change in relation to economic life and the ways in which goods and services are produced and consumed. These changes have been seen as particularly important in recent years because of their scale and magnitude, their impact upon everyday life and the primacy of knowledge and knowledge systems in these social changes. The changes that we have addressed are considered important by social scientists and, as we have shown, the social sciences have played a key role in both picking out these changes and in offering explanatory frameworks. We have looked at changes in the processes of production, for example the moves towards greater automization of the production processes, which have led to restructured social relations and altered working practices. In recent years fewer workers have been employed in manufacturing industries, although automization has permitted increased production of goods. This has led to the second shift that we have identified: the move from the primacy of production to an increased status for the point of consumption. More goods and services can be produced, thus opening up more possibilities for greater consumption. This move has also involved changes in the focus of explanations of social relations; a move from socio-economic class as the key determinant of social positioning to the notion of social status being shaped by patterns of consumption.

Both of these shifts have had important impacts upon what has been called the knowledge society. Increased automation involves the necessary acquisition of new skills by the workforce and a move from manual, physical skills towards a range of technical skills, which do not necessarily involve physical strength. More recently the skills and knowledge that have become most highly prized in the workplace are those involving new technologies and computer skills. Computerized technologies have challenged the requirements of place, in a world in which global networks now replace local industries and the speed of the transmission of knowledge has revolutionized many aspects of economic and social life. This knowledge revolution has incorporated changes in the valuing of knowledge. Although social scientists offer very different interpretations of the knowledge revolution, there is agreement about the primacy of knowledge and knowledge systems in the changes that have taken place, especially in recent years. What *is* disputed is the extent to which these changes have increased the control that we are able to exercise over our own lives. Does access to knowledge, at the click of a mouse, offer us more democratic participation in social and economic life or does it only provide a source of greater anxiety and distress? The availability of different, often competing sources of knowledge may create fears rather than allay them and we may be ill equipped to make judgements about competing perspectives on so many aspects of our daily lives. The availability of knowledge about risk may itself create fears, for example about disease, ill health and environmental danger because we have knowledge about possible disastrous outcomes in ways hitherto undreamed of.

Although there is some agreement about the centrality of knowledge in social changes in the late twentieth and early twenty-first centuries, there is dispute about the extent of the change. While the substance of knowledge may have changed it is the speed of transmission that carries the most impact, yet has the least substantial effect upon social relations. Changes in the structure of employment and the move from production to consumption do not themselves alter material circumstances, the distribution of power or access to resources. However, what is clear is that changes in knowledge systems and social changes are inextricably linked.

REFERENCES

Baudrillard, J. (1988) 'Consumer society' in Poster, M. (ed.) *Selected Writings*, Cambridge, Polity Press.

Bauman, Z. (2001) 'Consuming life', *Journal of Consumer Culture*, vol.1, no.1, pp.9–29.

Beck, U. (1995) *Ecological Politics in an Age of Risk*, Cambridge, Polity.

Beck, U. (1991) *Risk Society: Towards a New Modernity* (translated by Ritter, M.), London, Sage.

Bell, D. (1973) *The Coming of Post-Industrial Society*, London, Heinneman.

Bell, D. (1976) *The Cultural Contradictions of Capitalism*, London, Heinneman.

Cairncross, F. (1977) *The Death of Distance: How the Communications Revolution Will Change Our Lives*, London, Orion Business Press.

Daunton, M. and Hilton, M. (2001) *The Politics of Consumption*, Oxford, Berg.

du Gay, P. (ed.) (1997) *Production of Culture/Culture of Production*, London, Sage.

Hall, S. (ed.) (1997) *Representation*, London, Sage.

Held, D. (ed.) (2004) *A Globalizing World? Culture, Economics, Politics* (2nd edn), London, Routledge/The Open University.

Himmelweit, S. and Simonetti, R. (2004) 'Nature for Sale' in Hinchliffe, S. and Woodward, K. (eds) (2004) *The Natural and the Social: Uncertainty, Risk, Change* (2nd edition), London, Routledge/The Open University.

Lash, S. and Urry, J. (1994) *Economies of Signs and Space*, London, Sage.

Lasn, K. (2000) 'Culture jamming' in Schor, J. and Holt, D. (eds) *The Consumer Society Reader*, New York, The New Press.

Leadbeater, C. (1998) 'Welcome to the knowledge economy' in Hargreaves, I. and Christie, I. (eds) *Tomorrow's Politics: The Third Way and Beyond*, London, Demos.

Mackay, H. (2004) 'The globalization of culture?' in Held, D. (ed.)

Mackintosh, M. and Mooney, G. (2004) 'Identity, inequality and social class' in Woodward, K. (ed.) *Questioning Identity: Gender, Class, Ethnicity* (2nd edn), London, Routledge/The Open University.

Marx, K. and Engels, F. (1998) *The German Ideology*, London, Elecbook.

Rosenblatt, R. (ed.) (1999) *Consuming Desires*, Washington, Shearwater.

Taylor, T. and Tilford, D. (2000) 'Why consumption matters' in Schor, J. and Holt, D. (eds) *The Consumer Society Reader*, New York, The New Press.

FURTHER READING

Given the rather brief versions of the different theories of change that have been presented in this chapter, you could very usefully follow up the books cited here, for example by Daniel Bell, Ulrich Beck, Francis Cairncross and Scott Lash.

Anthony Giddens (1990) *The Consequences of Modernity*, Cambridge, Polity – provides a useful summary of some of the debates addressed in the chapter.

Frank Webster (2002) *Theories of the Information Society* (2nd edn) London, Routledge – is an excellent overview of issues raised by the knowledge society.

Juliet Schor and Douglas Holt (eds) (2000) *The Consumer Society Reader*, New York, The New Press – is another text that provides a summary of debates about the consumer society and the shift from production to consumption.

Afterword

David Goldblatt

In the Introduction to this book I posed five questions about knowledge and the social sciences which the subsequent chapters all attempted to address. What kind of balance sheet of answers, problems, and new questions can be drawn from their collective efforts? The answers to the first two of our five questions – what is knowledge?, and how is it socially constructed? – are reasonably straightforward. Knowledge is an organized and systematic collection of information, argument, skills, practices and understandings. Knowledge, in short, is a diverse, plural, multi-faceted phenomenon. However, knowledge includes the routine, everyday practices of what might be called 'common sense' and this common sense has a complex relationship with other forms of knowledge, including those that carry the status of more formal, institutional recognition. It can be sub-divided according to: its object of study; whether it exists in the form of theoretical, abstract systematic information or whether it is tacit, unreflective embodied skills and understandings of the world; and whether it is held in the mind of the knower or exists in some material form. As to its social construction, it would seem that the key issues raised in the Introduction have been borne out by the book. Language, institutions, social change and social problems all drive, shape and influence the content of any one knowledge system, its internal development, its relative social standing and legitimacy. Power operates at multiple, different points in the production of knowledge in all cases. The answers to our three other questions are more complex, tentative and uncertain.

The fate of expert and elite knowledges

In the Introduction I asked whether over the last half-century we have seen a significant decline in public trust in expert and elite knowledges. Trust is a notoriously hard thing to measure and track and much of the evidence that relates to this question in *Knowledge and the Social Sciences* is indirect. None the less, across the four chapters of the book a picture does emerge and it is a picture of *diversity*. In almost every field of knowledge there now exists a wider array of competing perspectives than existed in the immediate post-war era. Medical science must now compete for attention with complementary therapies and non-Western medical traditions. Mainstream Christianity must listen to and engage with the insistent and demographically significant voices of Islam, secularism and New Age cosmologies. The dominant political ideologies of the nineteenth and early twentieth centuries – conservatism, liberalism, social democracy and Marxism – have been confronted by new waves of articulate and powerful feminisms and environmentalisms. While these challenges and conflicts have been destabilizing and threatening for some, the plurality of argument and perspective available appears liberatory for others.

Alongside these *external* dialogues, both mainstream and peripheral, knowledge systems appear to be conducting intense and increasingly open internal dialogues. Of course, doctors, Christians and social democrats have never been uniform in their opinions and beliefs; there have always been internal debates, conflicts and schisms within these traditions. What, perhaps, distinguishes the contemporary era is the extent to which the general public is aware of those distinctions and divisions. Debates that were once confined to a small circle of influential figures and institutions within each of these traditions are now amplified through the enormously expanded means of communication that now exist. The media, in all its forms, has become less deferential in investigating such schisms, and more skilled and persistent in identifying and popularizing these debates. As a consequence, the general public has been exposed to the epistemological uncertainty that elite and expert knowledges and cultures have always possessed but rarely revealed. There has also been exposure to a vast array of different knowledges that can be transmitted at a speed that could not be imagined even 50 years ago. To put it bluntly: if the doctors/priests/politicians can't agree amongst themselves, why should we believe what they say? Diversity has become a source of uncertainty.

Can diversity and debate, both internal and external, account for these shifts alone? As I suggested above, the role of the modern media has been important in exposing to public view previously hidden or obscure disagreements and conflicts. But it seems unlikely that the media alone can account for the broad epistemological shifts we are charting. At least two other factors have been highlighted in *Knowledge and the Social Sciences*. Firstly, the public is, on balance, better educated, more literate, and more sophisticated and articulate than 40 or 50 years ago. The deference and hierarchies of an earlier era have been swept aside without new certainties and hierarchies being established. In short, the public is more receptive to and more able to comprehend the limits, failings and contradictions of elite and expert knowledge. Secondly, the efficacy and relevance of many expert and elite knowledge systems have been challenged on their own grounds. Conventional medicine has, by its own criteria of effective curative medicine, been found wanting. Iatrogenic diseases (illness caused directly by doctors and medical practices) have been identified in increasing numbers. The side effects and negative consequences of excessively pharmaceutical medicine, unnecessary and intrusive surgery, and the limits of the mind/body split that governs conventional medicine have all demonstrated the boundaries of medicine. Similarly, the capacity of conventional religious frameworks to deliver plausible, popular and coherent responses to complex practical and moral dilemmas in the modern world has been limited; from the ethics of family life, sexuality and divorce to abortion and genetic technologies, the moral arguments of conventional Christianity have had a slimmer purchase on the normative imaginations of much of the population of the UK. Political elites and their expert knowledges have also been challenged – the limits of contemporary representative democracy, and the limited capacity of national governing elites of whatever hue to deliver successful economic prosperity and social reform have undermined the powerful standing and authority of the dominant political traditions and representatives. In particular, the claim of states and politicians to deliver environmental security and safety has been undermined by the rising tide of environmental degradation, food scares, accidents and anxieties about the threats of global terrorism.

Knowledge and social change

From the above it should be clear that the development of new knowledge systems, and the conflicts within and between knowledge systems, can in itself be a factor in shaping and stimulating social change. Moreover, that change is not confined to the world of knowledge and culture alone but can cut deeply into the material and institutional structures of society. The advocates of the knowledge economy, in particular, suggest that new forms of scientific and marketing knowledge combined with new modes of communication and information processing are transforming Western societies. The balance between manufacturing and service industry and employment has been decisively shifted in favour of the service sector by new technologies and production processes. There has also been a shift in emphasis among social scientists from production to consumption as a key signifier and determinant of social relations. This in turn has led to a transformation of the system of social stratification in post-industrial societies and a redistribution of economic, cultural and political power. Advocates of post-Fordism and some post-modernists would of course argue that this account underplays the importance of pre-existing economic imperatives and institutions. The new technologies and knowledges can only have these kinds of effects in the context of a capitalist economy which shapes who owns, produces and deploys knowledge, and which relentlessly commodifies knowledge and information of all kinds treating it as one more form of inequitably distributed private property. Advocates of the risk society argue on the one hand that the creation and dissemination of information about new environmental risks and threats to human health and ecosystems do by themselves have major effects on social behaviour; knowledge of risk itself creates anxieties and uncertainties. On the other hand, the ways in which that information is produced, handled and debated cannot be divorced from the systems of environmental and safety regulation that we have inherited from industrial societies. It is only when new knowledge meets old institutions that social change and uncertainty begins.

Social change and the social sciences

What then has been the role of the social sciences in an era of social change and diversity? Have they been challenged by plausible and alternative explanations of the world from another quarter? Have they been a contributor to social change and, if so, in what way, in what combination, and in what kind of circumstance? On the basis of the book, we can only offer some very tentative reflections on these enormously complex issues, but they are, I think, a starting point for more concerted and sophisticated reflection. The social sciences can be seen to have played an important role in providing explanatory frameworks for understanding social change. These changes, as explored in this book, range across areas of experience from those of health care and our understanding of medicine to economic changes and the knowledge revolution. As we have seen the social sciences have been responsive to these changes and have played a part in providing the wider society with the language with which to make sense of change. The social sciences have always been exposed to internal division and diversity, as the debates in Chapter 2 over methodology (positivism and interpretative social science), in Chapter 3 over responding to environmental problems and in Chapter 4 over the trajectory of social change in response to the knowledge revolution, the consumer society and perceptions of risk, clearly demonstrate. That said, the promise of a social science that cannot merely describe and explain the world but, on the basis of such analysis, unproblematically deliver a programme of social reform and design tools of social change and intervention is discredited. The social sciences both in analysing the world and providing a means for intervention in the world, change and transform their object of study in unintended and unacknowledged ways that make their accounts avowedly problematic. Strategies of social engineering delivered solely from above and guided by neutral expert social scientists according to an already established blueprint are no longer tenable, as social scientists acknowledge.

Does this mean that the social sciences are redundant or irrelevant? On this point we can be more confident – they are not. The presentation of different explanatory frameworks is a major strength of the social sciences and is part of their responsiveness. What has emerged is the challenge to a 'grand theory', a single explanatory theory that can be applied to all situations at all times. The range of often competing perspectives, all implicated in responding to social change, is testimony to the flexibility and dynamism of the social sciences. The impossibility of simplistic social reform guided by a neutral and objective social science does not discredit the role of the social sciences and their transformative potential. Rather, it requires a more pluralist and diverse attitude to the process of social change and a more democratic form of the social sciences. In the increasingly complex and uncertain societies in which we live, the contemporary social sciences directly and indirectly provide the tools for more people and more social groups to engage in the process of social analysis and social change, in the evaluation and estimation of elites and experts, and in making the difficult choices that we individually and collectively face. If we have turned our backs on elite-led social change and elite interpretations of society then the future will be made by a much wider social constituency. This will require us to be more reflective about our own accounts of the world. It will also require us to be more insistent that with a potential cacophony of voices only democratic and open debate between competing positions can resolve the conflicts and choices we face. A passionate, open and critical knowledge of the social sciences is surely a central component of that debate and that future.

Acknowledgements

Grateful acknowledgement is made to the following sources for permission to reproduce material in this book.

Chapter 1

Text

Box 1.1: 'Feedback' column, *New Scientist*, vol.155 (2098), 6 September 1997, www.newscientist.com; Maddox, J. *et al.* (1988) '"High-dilution, experiments a delusion" Editorial Reservation'. *Nature,* no.333, June 1988, Macmillan Magazines Limited; Box 1.4: Adapted from 'Sudden death: the search for the truth about cot death'. *Horizon*, 25 February 1999. BBC TV.

Figures

Figure 1.2: John Harris/Report Digital; Figure 1.4: From: *Nouvelle Iconongraphie de la Saltpetriere* (1889) Paris, La Bibliotheque Charcot de la Saltpetriere; Figure 1.5: Contemporary Medical Archives Centre, Royal Army Medical Corps/Wellcome Institute Library, London; Figure 1.6: Mary Evans Picture Library/Fawcett Library; Figure 1.7: The Wellcome Trust Medical Photographic Library.

Chapter 2

Tables

Tables 2.1 and 2.3: Bruce, S. (1995) *Religion in Modern Britain*, Oxford University Press. Data: British Social Attitudes Survey, 1991; Table 2.2: Bruce, S. (1995) *Religion in Modern Britain*, Oxford University Press. Data: Gallup, G.H. (ed.) (1976) *The Gallup International Public Opinion Polls; Great Britain 1937–1975* (New York, Random House); Svennevig, M., Haldane, I., Speirs, S. and Gunter, B. (1989) *Godwatching: Viewers, Religion and Television* (London, John Libbey/IBA); Table 2.4: Davie, G. (1994) *Religion in Britain Since 1945*. Blackwell Publishers. Copyright © Grace Davie, 1994.

Figures

Figure 2.1: Front Cover of *Newsweek*, 12 July 1999. *'Is God Dead?'*. © 1999 Newsweek, Inc. All rights reserved. Reprinted by permission. Illustration by Mel Marcelo; Figure 2.2: 'Lost in silent prayer', *Newsweek*, vol.CXXXIII (2), 12 July 1999. © 1999 Newsweek, Inc. All rights reserved. Reprinted by permission; Figure 2.3: Bruce, S. (1995) *Religion in Modern Britain*, Oxford University Press; Figure 2.4: Brenda Prince/Format; Figure 2.5: Barry Hyam/Reform Synagogues of Great Britain; Figure 2.6: Peter MacDiarmid/*The Independent*; Figure 2.7: Nick Cobbing.

Chapter 3

Text

Reading 3.1: From *World Development Report, 1992*, World Bank, copyright ©
1992 by The International Bank for Reconstruction and Development/The World
Bank. Used by permission of Oxford University Press, Inc.; Reading 3.2: Arnold,
D. (1996) *The Problem Of Nature*, Blackwell Publishers.

Figures

Figure 3.1: Savran/Still Pictures; Figure 3.2: Nick Cobbing; Figures 3.3 and 3.8:
Still Pictures/Adrian Arbib; Figure 3.4: Still Pictures/Tim Rice; Figure 3.5:
© Greenpeace International Photolibrary; Figure 3.6: Service Photo de Parlement
European; Figure 3.7: Andrew Wiard/reportphoto.com.

Chapter 4

Figures

Figure 4.1: © Empics; Figure 4.2: © Sarah Lee/The Guardian; Figure 4.3: ©
National Motor Museum, Beaulieu; Figure 4.4: © Barbara Kruger. Courtesy: Mary
Boone Gallery, New York; Figure 4.5: Image courtesy www.adbusters.org.

Cover

Image copyright © 1996 PhotoDisc, Inc.

Every effort has been made to trace all copyright owners, but if any has been
inadvertently overlooked, the publishers will be pleased to make the necessary
arrangements at the first opportunity.

Index